The American Stage
and the Great Depression

The American Stage and the Great Depression: A Cultural History of the Grotesque proposes a correlation between the divided "mind" of America during the depression and popular stage works of the era. Theatre works such as Jack Kirkland's comic-horrific adaptation of *Tobacco Road*, Olsen and Johnson's "scream-lined revue" *Hellzapoppin*, and successful plays by Robert E. Sherwood, Clare Boothe Luce, and S. N. Behrman are interpreted as theatrical reflections of depression culture's sense of being trapped between a discredited past and a nightmarish future. The author analyzes the America of the 1930s as an era of the "grotesque," in which the irreconcilable were forced into tense and dynamic coexistence, and by examining these works of theatre as products of particular historical circumstances, argues for a strong connection between cultural history and theatre history.

CAMBRIDGE STUDIES IN AMERICAN THEATRE AND DRAMA

General Editor

Don B. Wilmeth, *Brown University*

Advisory Board

C. W. E. Bigsby, *University of East Anglia*
Errol Hill, *Dartmouth College*
C. Lee Jenner, *Independent Critic and Dramaturge, New York City*
Bruce A. McConachie, *College of William and Mary*
Brenda Murphy, *University of Connecticut*
Laurence Senelick, *Tufts University*

The American theatre and its literature are attracting, after long neglect, the crucial attention of historians, theoreticians, and critics of the arts. Long a field for isolated research, yet too frequently marginalized in the academy, the American theatre has always been a sensitive gauge of social pressures and public issues. Investigations into its myriad shapes and manifestations are relevant to students of drama, theatre, literature, cultural experience, and political development.

The primary aim of this series is to set up a forum for important and original scholarship in and criticism of American theatre and drama in a cultural and social context. Inclusive by design, the series accommodates leading work in areas ranging from the study of drama as literature to theatre histories, theoretical explorations, production histories, and readings of more popular or paratheatrical forms. While maintaining a specific emphasis on theatre in the United States, the series welcomes work grounded in cultural studies and narratives with interdisciplinary reach. *Studies in American Theatre and Drama* thus provides a crossroads where historical, theoretical, literary, and biographical approaches meet and combine, promoting imaginative research in theatre and drama from a variety of new perspectives.

BOOKS IN THE SERIES:

B. Dale Cockrell, *Demons of Disorder: Early Blackface Minstrels and Their World*
7. Rosemarie K. Bank, *Theatre Culture in America, 1825–1860*
6. Mark Fearnow, *The American Stage and the Great Depression*
5. Susan Harris Smith, *American Drama: The Bastard Art*
4. Jared Brown, *The Theatre in America during the Revolution*
3. Amy Green, *The Revisionist Stage: American Directors Reinvent the Classics*
2. Marc Robinson, *The Other American Drama*
1. Samuel Hay, *African American Theatre*

The American Stage and the Great Depression

A Cultural History of the Grotesque

MARK FEARNOW

The Pennsylvania State University

CAMBRIDGE
UNIVERSITY PRESS

PUBLISHED BY THE PRESS SYNDICATE OF THE UNIVERSITY OF CAMBRIDGE
The Pitt Building, Trumpington Street, Cambridge CB2 IRP, United Kingdom

CAMBRIDGE UNIVERSITY PRESS
The Edinburgh Building, Cambridge CB2 IRU, United Kingdom
40 West 20th Street, New York, NY 10011-4211, USA
10 Stamford Road, Oakleigh, Melbourne 3166, Australia

First published 1997

Printed in the United States of America

Typeset in Ehrhardt

Library of Congress Cataloging-in-Publication Data
The American stage and the Great Depression : a cultural history
of the grotesque / Mark Fearnow.
p.   cm. – (Cambridge studies in American theatre and drama)
Includes bibliographical references and index.
ISBN 0-521-56111-6 (hbk.)
1. American drama – 20th century – History and criticism.
2. Depressions – United States – History – 20th century.
3. Theater – United States – History – 20th century.
4. Depressions in literature.   5. Grotesque in literature.
I. Title.   II. Series
PS351.F44   1997
812'.5209358 – dc20   96–15493
CIP

A catalog record for this book is available from the British Library.

ISBN 0 521 56111 6 hardback

Contents

v

List of Illustrations

Acknowledgments

I AM DEEPLY GRATEFUL to the colleagues and mentors who offered advice at various stages of the preparation of this book. Tom Postlewait, Tim Wiles, Winona Fletcher, Rakesh Solomon, Bruce McConachie, Brenda Murphy, C.W.E. Bigsby, and Don Wilmeth were all superb readers of the text. Kim Fisher, of the Penn State Libraries, was valiant in dealing with some tricky research problems. Penn State's Institute for the Arts and Humanistic Studies assisted me at a crucial time with research funds, as did the School of Theatre Arts and its director, Dan Carter, and Ed Williams of the College of Arts and Architecture. Among the many copyright holders who have allowed me to quote from their material, I would particularly like to thank Joan Houseman for use of her late husband's memoirs. Maryann Chach and the Shubert Archive were generous in their permissions for photographs. My editors at Cambridge, T. Susan Chang and Anne Sanow, were accommodating throughout the process. Production editor Michael Gnat contributed greatly with his keen eye for detail. My thanks to all.

The turn lasted about fifteen minutes and during this time Riley and Robbins told some twenty jokes, beating Lem ruthlessly at the end of each one. For a final curtain, they brought out an enormous wooden mallet labeled "The Works" and with it completely demolished our hero. His toupee flew off, his eye and teeth popped out, and his wooden leg was knocked into the audience.

At the sight of the wooden leg, the presence of which they had not even suspected, the spectators were convulsed with joy. They laughed heartily until the curtain came down, and for some time afterwards.

Our hero's employers congratulated him on his success, and although he had a headache from their blows he was made quite happy by this. After all, he reasoned, with millions out of work he had no cause to complain.

– from the final chapter of
Nathanael West's *A Cool Million,* 1934

Introduction
Loving the Grotesque

If a painter should wish to unite a horse's neck to a human head, and spread a variety of plumage over limbs [of different animals] taken from every part [of nature], so that what is a beautiful woman in the upper part terminates unsightly in an ugly fish below – could you, my friends, refrain from laughter, were you admitted to such a sight?
— Horace, *The Art of Poetry*, 24–20 B.C.

THE MORNING OF 17 JUNE 1935 came on wet and gray as New Yorkers opened their papers at breakfast tables across the city and glanced through the headlines. Amid the stories of President Roosevelt's new work program, which was to provide three hundred million dollars for the employment of white-collar workers – and even included plans to employ artists, writers, and actors – were less portentous stories that nevertheless attracted the reader's eye. Members of the fashionable Mayfair Country Club, atop Eagle Rock in West Orange, New Jersey, were recovering from the excitement of the shooting death of a young gangster in their bar the previous evening. The gunman had recognized one of the five detectives who had come to the club to arrest him and, leaving a young blond woman at his table, had drawn his pistol. Before the gunman could fire, Captain William Wylie of the West Orange police drew his revolver and fired a shot that struck the man – Vincent Diauon, age twenty-seven – in the head. Diauon turned and attempted to flee the barroom, just as the officer fired again, the bullet striking Diauon in the back. Still struggling ahead, Diauon made it out of the bar and across the foyer to a small dining room, where he collapsed and died. Over a hundred people were in the bar at the time of the shooting, and about twenty couples were on the dance floor as the band, playing "She's My Cookie," brought the music to "an abrupt halt."[1]

The adjacent headlines announced other compelling stories. Michel Fokine's mansion on Riverside Drive had been burglarized to the tune of twenty-five thousand dollars worth of jewelry and minks. One brooch was itself valued at ten thousand dollars. Two people had drowned when they had rowed out to look at Admiral Byrd's Antarctic exploring vessel in Jamaica Bay and their boat had capsized, and in Jamaica, Queens, three boys who ranged in age from eleven to thirteen had stolen a gun from a policeman's coat and "embarked on a career of crime." They had first tried to rob a woman on the street, but she had slapped their faces and sent them on their way. They moved on to a nearby lot where they found William Walsh, age thirty-six, asleep in the grass. They woke him, and when he refused to turn over his money, the boys shot him in the head, killing him instantly. One of the older boys, Lisbon Lawrence, was the son of the Reverend Edward Lawrence, pastor of the Mount Calvary Baptist Church.[2]

Turning past the front page, readers would have glanced through the announcements on entertainment. There was to be another air show on the weekend. There was plenty of action in boxing and baseball. Earl Carroll's new *Sketchbook* was in its third week at the Winter Garden. Leslie Howard and Humphrey Bogart were still in *The Petrified Forest* at the Broadhurst, and the Theatre Guild was continuing a left-wing revue called *Parade* that wasn't expected to run much longer. Many of the New York readers would already have seen *Three Men on a Horse* and *Anything Goes. The Children's Hour* was giving its 249th performance that night.

As the morning advanced and the rain outside turned to a fine mist, many would have closed their papers and glanced again at the front-page stories before heading off to begin the day. Some would decide to see *Tobacco Road* again that night. For many it would be the third time.

Theatre and Culture

The Swiss theologian Karl Barth once counseled preachers to approach the pulpit with the Scriptures in one hand and the day's newspaper in the other. A similar, though more athletic, approach seems necessary for those who hope to understand theatre as a part of cultural history – to juggle at once the slippery "facts" of an era and the even more elusive "facts" of the theatre of the period and to keep them suspended together in some sort of wobbly orbit. There is always the danger of dropping one set on the floor.

The American theatre of the Great Depression – here taken from 1930 through 1941, by which time the massive gears of war production were grinding out a new economy and a new set of national obsessions, was a specialized mirror of the national consciousness. The theatre is too complex an art for simple reflection. The vast variety in status, location, ideology, and plain artistic ability in producers of theatre is dwarfed by the astonishing problem of audiences and their situation and motivation within culture. Both of these are set within the shifting matrix of a culture that, at first glance, appears to possess an unlimited ability to contradict itself.

In spite of these complexities, patterns do emerge from these encounters with the past. Siegfried Kracauer (in *From Caligari to Hitler*) and Mikhail Bakhtin (in *Rabelais and His World*) offer ways of understanding an art as a function of culture and as indicators of what Kracauer calls the "mentality" of a nation. These studies are convincing because they strike a balance between the analysis of text and of cultural context, a method that avoids the aesthetic myopia that is the danger of exclusively text-based analyses as well as the statistical imprecision and exaggerated "objectivity" of more recent "reception" approaches. Of course, the writer who takes up literature or film may find the job somewhat easier, as the objects of their researches at least have the good manners to stay put so that the researcher can read them or watch them in largely the same form as those who first read or watched them and who participated in the social adventure of their making. The objects of theatre, however, like the age that produced them, have disappeared, and we are left with photographs that may be misleading, reviews that were meant to sell papers, and descriptions of what people think they saw. To create a meaning from these materials requires a double intention: to admit at once a selection from the sea of "facts" in the service of one's intuition and, at the same time, to discipline that selection by applying to it a larger intellectual construct of the cultural motions of the period. It is a creative job, more like a novelist's than a social scientist's, because the critic is leaping from "data" to a reconstruction that amounts to a narrative. It is the telling of the story of the age.

A Social Theory of the Grotesque

To any consideration of depression America, we bring the images already etched in our minds. We see breadlines and apple sellers in their inevitable urban streets, grainy and in low-contrast black and white. We see police bashing strikers in blurry stills from newsreels and lean "Okies" looking worried, though perfectly framed within pleasing compositions. We see dust bowls and Roosevelt and Shirley Temple, the NRA eagle on a storefront and Tom Joad crouching in a ditch. We think of a thunderstruck audience at the opening night of *Waiting for Lefty* and of a cool and intelligent Hallie Flanagan defending the Federal Theatre against philistine politicians. These images and hundreds more of comparable power and durability compete for the role of defining icon.

If one becomes more systematic and studies the headlines of the newspapers of the era in search of the topics that most fascinated newspaper buyers, a quintet of obsessions emerges: Hitler, Roosevelt, Lindbergh and flying, gangsters, and the movies. Highly sensational narratives were the norm for even the most "serious" newspapers and, after reading several hundred of them, one notices a peculiar, persistent characteristic in the tone and structure of these stories. It is the same characteristic that crops up again and again in many of the most successful theatre productions of the era, as well as in the films, radio drama, sport, and other entertainments. It is the grinning face of the grotesque.

What has come to be called "the grotesque" has existed from the time of the earliest narratives and cave paintings, and critics have often noted its special abundance in the art of cultures that are experiencing intense stress and social anxiety. The concept itself has been adapted within the past century to our special need to describe objects that sustain in tension ideas or styles or points of view that are contradictory and that, consequently, provoke an ambivalent response in the perceiver. The grotesque is thus the hallmark of depression America. It is the one critical idea that can take in the absurd contrasts of a country in a time when it is both broken down with misery and despair, and brimming over with a perky native boosterism; resplendent and self-aware of its status as the first technological age, and cringing with fear at the changes that technology had wrought; looking forward with a utopian eye to "The World of Tomorrow," and hearkening back with a quaint nostalgia to a horse-drawn and gaslit age that lay only a couple of decades in the past. The grotesque is the one critical idea that explains the theatre of a period offering the astonishing twin successes of *Life with Father* and *Tobacco Road*. The grotesque is the one name for a social machine capable of taking in the horrific materials of a world spinning toward conflagration, mixing them with the commonplace and the comic, and producing objects that one could look at and then know – objects that may have been troubling but that nevertheless had been tamed.

Every writer on the grotesque since the birth of the word (from a hole beneath the streets of late-fifteenth-century Rome, wherein workers found a Roman grotto filled with paintings of absurdly conflated plants and animals) has considered the grotesque as contradiction inside of a work of art.[3] The now-classic applications by John Ruskin (*The Stones of Venice*, 1851), Wolfgang Kayser (*The Grotesque in Art and Literature*, 1957), and Mikhail Bakhtin (*Rabelais and His World*, 1940) form a unity with more recent Freudian approaches in analyzing the work of art as an indicator of contradiction in a whole culture.[4] When one's rummaging in the cultural junk heap goes farther afield to include both art and less "artistic" cultural artifacts, the grotesque reveals itself as an amazing kind of animal that can appear and disappear, winding its way in and out of the cracks in the wall that separates life from its representation in art, smiling from behind the words of the news report, and tempting the artist to catch him. The grotesque is not only a result of random playfulness on the part of the artist or artisan; it is the representation of the "not-making-sense" that people perceive in the world around them, a perception that is pervasive in times of rapid social change and to which the people of such an age become especially sensitive.

The word "grotesque," taken up enthusiastically by Renaissance commentators, rapidly grew from a narrow referencing of one set of Roman paintings to a whole "type" of art and then to an overarching critical idea because it provided the linguistic tool to describe not just an ingredient that they had noticed in art, but also moments of their own experience. In Renaissance Europe, the word described the countless instances of incongruous juxtaposition that occurred as an old "mentality," based in the philosophical assumptions of Christian dogma and the practical acceptance of ecclesiastical power, gave way in erratic stages to a new mentality rooted in notions of science and temporal power. Such moments were, as they are now, persistent in their demand for attention. They do not fit into the regular forms that art and reason provide for the processing of experience, the forms by which we order our lives and convert experience into meaning. A tragic form provides a structure for finding meaning in our moments of suffering or ecstasy; a comic form makes meaning from experiences of abandonment and insight. Historical moments like the Renaissance or the Great Depression, however, are rife with experiences that do not fit into those structures. Nevertheless, people feel the ancient need to represent these troubling experiences in some way so that they might feel the tentative assurance of control over experience that representation provides. Their efforts take the form of the unresolved mixing that appears to the critical eye as "grotesque."

Depression America provides a rich field for an analysis of the relation of grotesque art and artifacts to the events of the age and to other simultaneous cultural signs. The experience of rapid conversion to a technological world, coupled with the devastation of the economy and the growing threat of a new world war, produced a sensitivity to what might be called a "sense" of the grotesque in large numbers of people. This same sense led those whose role it was to represent "reality" in whatever form to give special emphasis to incongruous juxtapositions in their work; thus, the historical situation of depression America led to a widespread sense of the grotesque that found voice in cultural signs as diverse as the narrative style of news reports, the structure and content of commercial plays, and the rise of the horror film in Hollywood. Within this particular cultural context, these grotesque objects achieved a relative popularity that is historically unusual.

Flannery O'Connor frequently expressed her frustration that "anything that comes out of the South is going to be called grotesque by the Northern reader, unless it is grotesque, in which

case it is going to be called realistic."[5] Few culture makers of
the depression set out to create "grotesque" representations.
With the exception of highly self-conscious artists like William
Faulkner and Nathanael West, artists and other chroniclers of
depression America set out to represent "reality" in a way that
seemed true (in the sense of accurately descriptive) to them or
– as in the case of Tod Browning and other directors of horror
films – to represent the fantastic. Of course, the assumptions
that form the foundation for a study seeking a link between the
"mind" of a culture and its products are that the makers of
cultural artifacts were at least unconsciously affected by the
social history of their time and that their works are irremedi-
ably marked by that history.

If the representation of "not-making-sense" does provide
audiences with Freudian "pleasure" (relief), it would seem –
following the principles of the Frankfurt School – that the grotesque object works to buttress the dominant ideology. As a
force that reduces the fears of the bourgeois ego, grotesque art
would thus be seen as a narcotizing tool of patriarchal capitalism, and notions of the disruptive power of the grotesque would
make little sense.

A solution to the problem of how the grotesque can both relieve anxiety and oppose the dominant ideology lies in a distinction about the kind of pleasure it provides. The pleasure that
we feel in the representation of the experiences we call "grotesque" is highly limited. The grotesque is unlike the mythic
categories of comedy and tragedy in that it fixes experience
but does not convert it to meaning. A grotesque representation
provides a degree of distance from a contradictory moment but
it does not resolve the contradiction. The grotesque object offers a kind of box in which to place the odd moment so that
we can go on with life, but it does not allow us to bundle the

package and put it neatly away with the label, "Here I experienced suffering," as the tragic form might do or, "Here I saw the way of the world and laughed," as we might in deriving meaning through the comic form. Instead, the "box" of the grotesque is always on the front shelf of our consciousness, labeled but always open, and has things moving around inside.

Thus, the grotesque object does not narcotize its audience because it does not allow them to be easily finished with the experience of observing it. When a grotesque performance has "happened" for an audience, they do not leave the space feeling "good" in the sense of experiencing a sentimental satisfaction. The comic tango between Hitler and Stalin featured in the 1939 edition of the long-running *Pins and Needles* (Figure 1), a leftish satirical revue, is emblematic of the tension in grotesquerie: The dance is funny, but at the same time generates a feeling of anxiety. We pretend, as an audience, that we have the tyrants captive here before us, our puppets, dancing fools; but behind the rigid poses and frozen expressions arise in our imaginations specters – the real Hitler, the physical Stalin, powerful and deadly, furious at this scene of mockery. We laugh in our dark theatre but feel the imprint of fear, or – to reverse the metaphor – see around the mockery the halo of a potential retribution. An incongruity has been represented, but not resolved.

Tania Modleski points to a similar phenomenon in her convincing analysis of contemporary horror films.[6] Whereas the Frankfurt School saw "mass culture" as a monolithic construct, solidly aligned with the dominant ideology, Modleski points to the possibility of subtlety and contradiction within that culture, even in so "top-directed" and seemingly "industrial" an arena as Hollywood cinema. She demonstrates how films like *The Texas Chainsaw Massacre, Dawn of the Dead,* and *Halloween* –

Figure I. Jesting with the horrific: Hitler (Berni Gould) and Stalin (Harry Clark) were spoofed in "Five Little Angels of Peace" from the 1939 edition of Labor Stage's *Pins and Needles*. (New York Public Library)

grotesque objects all – attack every institution of bourgeois culture and turn "pleasure" to an oppositional use: The films abandon the usual narcissistic identification of audience with character and its consequent "narrative pleasure" in favor of a "joyful self-destructiveness" on the part of the audience. These works are, then, "just as apocalyptic and nihilistic, as hostile to meaning, form, pleasure, and the specious good" as the forms of "high art" that are usually identified as disruptive forces in culture (p. 162).

Modleski's insights apply equally well to grotesque objects of the depression. Works that refuse to assume an accepted form (like *Idiot's Delight*) or sustain the audience in a tension between pathos and comedy (like *Tobacco Road*), or create a Dionysiac confusion within the space (like *Hellzapoppin*) offer a disruption of Adorno's "spurious harmony" and a denial of "ego-reinforcement" in a way similar to that of the horror films of the 1980s. In both cases, the grotesque work operates within the structure of mass culture but avoids the usual functions of narcotization and containment.

With these principles in mind, we can formulate a definition of the grotesque that will serve as a critical tool in the study of culture: The word "grotesque" refers to one's apprehension of an unresolved contradiction among two or more elements in an object, producing within one a sense of tension that nevertheless resolves into a limited pleasure in finding similar conflicts from life to have been "named." The grotesque object thus operates as part of a social "machine" that transforms vague anxieties and discordant fears of a culture into forms in which they are represented and mingled with comic elements. Thus reified, these cultural "nightmares" are rendered less frightening but remain troubling and disruptive of an easy acceptance of "reality"; the grotesque object instead holds those who perceive it in a horrified fascination, as in the case of children who gather around to look at a bat in a mayonnaise jar. The bat, which only moments before had been the source of terror as it swooped over their heads, has been converted to a "funny monster," and – like a comedy about the end of the world or a campy film about werewolves – the glass jar holds the terror at bay, a visible and captured thing, baring its teeth at the onlookers and hissing away in vain.

I

The Grotesque and
the Great Depression

. . . and what are poets for in a destitute time?
— from Hölderlin's "Bread and Wine,"
quoted by Heidegger in *Poetry, Language, Thought*

IN A POLITICAL SPEECH OF 1934, President Franklin
Delano Roosevelt looked back on the events of recent history and declared that the stock market crash had brought
a just but bitter end to "the crazy decade" of 1919–29.[1] During
those years, he declared, "the wheels of democracy had failed
to function" and society permitted "vast sections of our population to exist in an un-American way." His "New Deal" was
to be no temporary measure, but a rebuilding of America in
such a way that "never again" would such conditions exist.

Roosevelt was by no means alone in this perspective on the
past. Throughout the detritus of the Great Depression one
finds expressed directly or in subtextual statements the belief
that the twenties had been a kind of cultural orgy that had cul-

minated in the crash of 1929 and for which the depression was
severe but just payment. Allied with this overarching belief
were two subsidiary ones: that the crash signified not only the
economic failure of society, but also the failure of all of its institutions, and that the present moment demanded either a
starting over or a return to the traditions of the past. What had
seemed like brave exploration in the twenties – industrializa-
tion, sexual liberation, artistic experimentation – seemed to
many to have led only to disaster; in their eyes, the people of
the thirties stood among the relics of a ruined world.

People who perceive themselves as standing amid ruins can
be expected to look in one of two directions. In one direction
lies what they see as a creative option: The destruction of the
old world is taken as an opportunity to start over and make a
better one. The energy here is forward looking, and its adherents advocate new political and economic systems, new mores
and new art, all of which take advantage of the latest in technology and learning and are suitable for what the people of the
depression called "modern life." Around this pole one may
cluster such phenomena of depression America as the left-wing
movement in politics; "Reform" politics; the New Deal, including its expression in the creation of public buildings, dams,
and forests and in more obvious cultural expressions such as
the Federal arts projects; aviation and polar exploration; public
fascination with physics in general and with Albert Einstein in
particular; and modern design in architecture, automobiles, and
consumer products.

This rhetoric of progress sounded as appealing to the American ear in the thirties as it does today. Images of growth and
discovery are basic building blocks in the country's idea of itself. However, a futuristic vision also carries with it a burden
of anxiety. Such a course involves the total reliance on our own

creativity. Without reliance upon the defeated past, the techno-optimist looks toward the new things that we make up to run the world, and these new things could fail. Their failure could destroy us utterly.

In another direction lies the way of retreat into nostalgia, or – to express it more positively – a reliance on tradition. Here hope takes the form of dogmas and imagery from a past epoch in which culture was, at least from a present perspective, organized and meaningful. This stance is generally less attractive to Americans than is the futurist one, but the nostalgist option does harmonize with other parts of the American myth, as is demonstrated in its adherents' use of such language as "the American way of life," "traditional values," "plain common sense," and other patriotic and agrarian expressions.

Many in depression America made use of the theme of rejuvenating the present by a return to "old ways," traditions that carried with them not only the practical attribute of being "tried and true" but also a sort of mystic power, a sacredness that had been violated when these values were lost and that now must be reclaimed. Americans were called to return to the covenant that – in the national myth – had made them great. The impulse found its most appealing expression in the agrarian movement and the films of Frank Capra, but it is also prominent in the rhetoric and policies of the Hoover administration; FDR's dream of a new agrarianism, expressed most clearly in the Civilian Conservation Corps; the enormous fascination with the book and film versions of *Gone with the Wind;* the renewed interest in Americana, including not only the flood of books, plays, and films about American history (especially Abraham Lincoln), but also the popularity of antique collecting and the building of "Colonial Williamsburg" by the Rockefellers; the brief and enormous popularity of reactive figures

such as Father Coughlin, Dr. Townsend, and Huey Long; the
national fascination with Hitler and Mussolini and their dreams
of rebuilding great cultures of the past; and the widespread interest in "historical pageants" in rural communities.

This spiritual crisis of the 1930s was abundantly document-
ed by the sociologists Robert S. Lynd and Helen Merrell Lynd.
The radical, forced schism between traditional notions and
modern realities became the dominant theme of their fascinating 1935–6 study, *Middletown in Transition: A Study in Cultural Conflicts.*[2] In this book, the Lynds and their research team
returned to Muncie, Indiana, a town that they had selected a
decade earlier as being, statistically, the "average American in-
land town." *Middletown,* their 1925 book reporting the results
of the original study, had become a surprise best-seller, with
its tables of demographic statistics and voting records shored
up by the Lynds' factual and dramatic verbal portrait of a typical midwestern town.[3] Now the sociologists wanted to see how
the town had changed as a result of the depression and technological pressures. Middletown had always been driven by a
an overarching belief in "progress," a belief system that had
worked well for its citizens during the 1920s as the town's
economy turned away from agriculture and toward manufactur-
ing. These business–oriented ideals were the foreground to a
religious background that adapted Christianity into a kind of
booster club for money-making and that was itself making "religious progress" (pp. 295–318). With the coming of massive unemployment and industrial near-collapse, the ideals of unend-
ing "growth" and both industrial and theological "progress"
were under serious threat. As the Lynds put it, "Middletown
busily turned its wishes into horses – and then abruptly and
helplessly rode them over a precipice" (p. 3).

By 1935, people were scrambling to plaster over the ideological cracks. People of the town were "uneasily conscious of
many twinges down under the surface," but they struggled to
suppress this intuition, as in the case of a person who insists
on "denying and disregarding unpleasant physical symptoms
on the theory that everything must be all right, and that if anything really is wrong it may cure itself without leading to a major operation" (p. 490). Yet the crisis persisted, the individual's
mind goaded away from the comfort of the naïve values of the
past but afraid of the "radicalism" offered by new social and
ideological systems:

One suspects that for the first time in their lives many Middletown
people have awakened, in the depression, from the sense of being at
home in a familiar world to the shock of living as an atom in a universe dangerously too big and blindly out of hand. With the falling
away of literal belief in the teachings of religion in recent decades,
many Middletown folk have met a similar shock, as the simpler universe of fifty years ago has broken up into a vastly complicated physical order. (p. 491)

Americans of Middletown represent a culture of the thirties
that can be understood as a crisis in the omnipresent conflict
between the futurist and nostalgist positions. As the Lynds
suggest, these tensions were not new in the 1930s, but the drastic economic events of the depression brought them to a head.
If Americans' sense of being caught in a time of tension between a failed past and a frightening future is the core "reality" around which depression culture was built, the solution
that the Lynds saw the people of Middletown applying to this
schism will have its cultural manifestations: "[T]hey have been
able," the Lynds wrote in 1936, "to retain the shadowy sense

of their universe's being in beneficent control by the common expedient of believing themselves *to live in a world of unresolved duality*" (p. 491 [italics added]). This is the strategy of the grotesque. Americans of the 1930s were torn between looking forward and back. "People want to live hopefully and adventurously into the future," the Lynds wrote, "but if the future becomes too hazardous they look steadily toward the known past" (p. 493). It was this desire to see duality manifested that led to the creation of so many grotesque objects during the 1930s, and it was the reification of this tension, of opposites held temporarily together, that provided people of Middletown and elsewhere the pleasure they felt in viewing grotesque objects.[4]

Gone with the Wind

Also attractive to mass audiences in the thirties were texts that seemed to eliminate the cultural conflict between future and past that grotesque works kept in dynamic action. It was possible to portray the split in directions as having been imaginary in the first place, the illusion of a confused antagonist. *Gone with the Wind,* the most successful single text in the mass culture of the period, offers just such a resolution in its final pages. Scarlett O'Hara – who has operated throughout the book as a figure torn between the social mores of the Old South and the new pragmatism and commercial brutality of Reconstruction – stands crushed and abandoned in the foyer of her lavish and modern home in the big city. Her "modern" urban life – of an assertive businesswoman – had seemingly collapsed around her, but then a thought occurs to her, a "bulwark against the rising tide of pain":

"I'll – why, I'll go home to Tara tomorrow," and her spirits lifted faintly. . . . She had gone back to Tara once in fear and defeat and had emerged from its sheltering walls strong and armed for victory. What she had done once, somehow – please God, she could do again! How, she did not know. She did not want to think of that now. All she wanted was a breathing space in which to hurt, a quiet place to lick her wounds, a haven in which to plan her campaign. . . . And Mammy would be there. Suddenly she wanted Mammy desperately, as she had wanted her when she was a little girl, wanted the broad bosom on which to lay her head, the gnarled black hand on her hair. Mammy, the last link with the old days.[5]

In this section, as throughout the narrative, Scarlett O'Hara can be seen as a stand-in for depression America, and her struggle in the chaos of the Civil War and Reconstruction a portrayal of the country's struggle in the depression and New Deal, translated to the level of myth. In the course of the novel Scarlett moves from being a frivolous and selfish woman-child, preoccupied with a fantasy world of barbecues and flirtation that she assumed would go on forever (the "orgy" of the twenties) to a true adulthood, forged in the adversity of the war and its aftermath (the depression of the early thirties). Like Scarlett, America could return to its "Tara," the body of myth and tradition symbolized by such projects as Rockefeller's Williamsburg, and from this haven plan its campaign. The flight to the comfort in nostalgia is taken farther and personified in the figure of Mammy, who serves as a kind of cosmic mother figure, the "last link with the old days," her "broad bosom" the cushion of national "heritage" and myth upon which the country should recline.

This passage offers the key to decoding the ideology of the book, the popular appeal of which is evidenced by the astonishing profitability of the book and the film that followed it three years later. It is an ideology that turns on a rhetorical strategy of avoidance: Culture does not have to make the radical choice between the old world and the new; rather, it can retreat into the past as a palliative while it decides what to do. Margaret Mitchell's solution to her crisis represents a sort of suspended animation in which culture can rest while it gets its "thoughts" straight. Like Scarlett O'Hara, America can "think about it all tomorrow."[6]

Political Rhetoric

The cultural texts of depression America that rivaled *Gone with the Wind* as objects of national fascination and identification came from the world of politics. Newspapers routinely printed the texts of political speeches, and the rhetoric of these politicians – their definition of the current crisis and the proper course of action – were essential in the country's idea of itself. Franklin Delano Roosevelt and Adolf Hitler, the two looming figures of the era, described the crisis of a world caught between ages. Their speeches did not offer tradition as a haven but turned instead on the image of a synthesis of the past with the future. The popularity of this strategy is evidenced by the propulsion of the two men not just to political power in their own countries, but to the status of larger-than-life symbolic personas, each connected with his own vast system of highly charged cultural signs.

The case of Hitler is especially telling. Many Americans of the early 1930s found Hitler and his rhetoric to have a powerful appeal. Reports of his speeches and actions in American newspapers often communicated a subtext of admiration for Hitler's boldness and efficiency, as in the *New York Times* references to his "swift and decisive actions" in executing Roehm and other homosexual officers in July of 1934.[7] A month later, the *Times* reporter referred to Hitler's action as a "cleansing."[8]

If Hitler's rhetoric was geared to appeal to a German culture in collapse, the rhetoric of FDR worked a similar synthesis in the United States. Both leaders managed to look in two directions at once and by doing so captured the imaginations of large segments of their populations. Both Hitler and Roosevelt promised to re-create the glories of their nations' pasts while appropriating what was useful from the modern epoch. In making this linkage of old and new, they managed an ideological synthesis that seemed to many to have solved the problem of what to do in a world that was breaking down.

In a speech to the Nazi congress in September 1934, Hitler described National Socialism as a "world philosophy" that was "not only the expression of a political system and reform of the State, but also a reshaping of personal, communal, and cultural life."[9] This cultural movement was a rejection of "Jewish intellectualism" and a return, in the words of the *New York Times* correspondent, to "intuition and an organic conception of civilization." Continuing his summary of the speech, the reporter noted:

As a cultural movement, he believed, it was faced by two dangers. On the one hand it was menaced by the intrusion of busybodies who hawked about newfangled ideas regardless of their cost. On the other hand, there were unproductive imitators of past forms of expression, which, though respected by National Socialism, were unsuitable for imitation. The Greeks, Herr Hitler said, were akin to the National Socialists.

Roosevelt's rhetoric of his first term offered this same synthesis of past greatness with modern efficiency. He promised both a "New Deal" and a restoration of the "temple of our civilization" to the "ancient truths."[10] In his second inaugural address, Roosevelt described the work of the previous four years as bringing the "private autocratic powers" that had made a mockery of the Constitution "into their proper subordination to the people's government."[11] He then elaborated:

But that is not all that you and I mean by the new order of things. Our pledge was not merely to do a patchwork job with second-hand materials. By using the new materials of social justice, we have undertaken to erect on the old foundations a more enduring structure for the better use of future generations. . . . Old truths have been relearned, untruths have been unlearned. . . . We are beginning to wipe out the line that divides the practical from the ideal, and in so doing we are fashioning an instrument of unimagined power for the establishment of a morally better world.

Though Hitler and Roosevelt obviously differed radically in the content and methods of their reforms, both placed themselves, "the people," and the ancients on one side and recent corrupters of the ancient way on the other. Whereas Hitler relied on racist and anti-Semitic sentiments to reinforce this union, Roosevelt relied on popular hatred of nameless "money-changers" and "self-seekers" in the "temple." The success of these strategies offers a key to an understanding of the essential tension of the period, a sense that people shared of being caught between eras, or – as Elmer Rice's play called it – *Between Two Worlds*. An age of horses and royalty was bumping into an age of airplanes, television, and air-conditioning, an incongruous juxtaposition that created a widespread sense of the grotesque from which people sought relief in politics and in art.

The "Survival"

In any period of radical transition, people and institutions from the past survive into a present in which they have no apparent place, and – like Irving's Rip Van Winkle – they stand looking about, glassy-eyed, confused and blinking at a bewildering scene. Reports of their activities attract attention and jump out from the pages of newspapers:

Primo's Son Fights Duel with Captain; Both Slightly Wounded in Second Encounter

PAMPLONA, Spain, March 3. [1930] –

Meeting here secretly yesterday morning, Miguel Primo de Rivera, son of the former Spanish dictator, and Captain Rexach of the Spanish Artillery Corps fought a duel with swords in which each was slightly wounded. Miguel was cut once in the wrist and Captain Rexach was cut twice.

They separated when the seconds ruled that Captain Rexach's cuts on the wrist were too serious to permit of his continuing the duel, but apparently they were not reconciled. It is rumored that they want to fight again.

Miguel came from Paris where he was staying with his father and other members of his family, and slipped over the frontier by automobile through a pass in the Pyrenees. . . . Young Miguel was recently sent out of Spain to prevent his fighting duels. He had challenged several officers whom he accused of having insulted his father, slapping a General publicly in one of Madrid's most fashionable cafes. . . .[12]

In addition to the obvious note of romance that the reporter hoped to convey in this piece of reporting is a strong sense of the comic in the depiction of Miguel Primo de Rivera go-

ing about Spain – a country on the verge of a civil war that
would be fought with machine guns and aerial bombardments
– slapping generals in cafés and fighting officers with a sword.
There is also a sense of the grotesque in the image of a duel-
ist, a figure we associate with the manners of previous centuries, riding in an automobile. The image of the "young Miguel"
is at once dashing and absurd, and his story is essentially pathetic.

These "survivals" from a previous era – a term supplied by
the Jewish refugee from fascism in S. N. Behrman's *Rain from
Heaven* (1934) – present themselves in news reports. What is
fascinating to find in observing these reports is that journalists
frequently emphasized grotesque collisions, highlighting peculiar details of the case that were hardly essential to the narrative. When fire threatened to destroy Sagamore Hill, the home
of the late President Theodore Roosevelt, it was reported that
his widow, "who never left the house, directed her servants to
serve coffee and cakes to the firemen."[13] James Brandon, orig-
inally a resident of Nashville, Tennessee, died in Poona, India,
from "a broken heart" because he had lost the "magic spectacles" he believed had given him the power of "divine healing,"
for which he had been known in that area for fifteen years.[14]
New York Mayor Jimmy Walker, returning from a "rest cure"
in Germany in the midst of the many scandals that eventually led to the defeat of Tammany Hall by LaGuardia's reform
movement, said that "One must laugh on the stage of politics
no matter what the sadness within."[15] Three years later, a surviving symbol of Tammany's reign was attacked as LaGuardia's
park commissioner demanded the closing of the Central Park
Casino as "an improper and illegal use of the premises in a
public park."[16]

The absurd situation of these "survivals," persons caught inside an incongruity, did not go unnoticed by intellectuals and artists. They were observed and represented in forms ranging from the "primitive" old folks who embarrass the younger and mannered planters by belching at the Wilkeses' barbecue in *Gone with the Wind* (1938) to Chaplin's little tramp, thrown into jail every time he expresses some human quality in his various jobs in *Modern Times* (1936).

The artist who may have been most keenly aware of this problem, or at least most articulate in defining it, was the playwright Robert E. Sherwood. Sherwood suffered mightily in his contemplation of the end of Western civilization as the world had known it, and he made this gigantic crisis the obsessive theme of his work in the 1930s, a theme he elaborated in long and anguished prefaces to the published plays. *Reunion in Vienna* (Figure 2), an admittedly light farce that Sherwood crafted for the Lunts and the Theatre Guild, is described in his preface as "another demonstration of the escape mechanism in operation." Sherwood felt that his generation was occupying "the limbo–like interlude between one age and another."[17] The collapse of religion left only science as an alternative, and this child of rationalism had turned into a "monster" (p. x). Both the "discredited vicars of God" and the "discredited ideologues of the laboratory" are scorned because humankind believes that it was the scientists "who got [them] into this mess" (p. xi). The "modern" human is left in an impossible position, unable to return to faithful innocence and terrified of a science that has brought the world more destruction than life. If the generation of the 1930s has any descendants (rather than the "laboratory products" that Sherwood fears science will enable), they face a meaningless, beliefless existence. Thus he and his kind are survivals: the last children of an age that believed naïvely in Progress, living on now, humanist wanderers in a world of antihumanism. "It would seem," Sherwood wrote, "that the only subjects now available for man's contemplation are his disillusionment with the exposed past and his disinclination to accept the stultifying circumstances of the revealed future" (pp. xiv–xv). Sherwood's plays through most of the decade dramatize these demoralized pilgrims. The deposed aristocrats of *Reunion in Vienna* (1931), the hitchhiking poet who sacrifices himself before the forces of chaos in *The Petrified Forest* (1935), and the stranded entertainer and phony princess in *Idiot's Delight* (1936) are all pathetic, ridiculous, courageous misfits among the new barbarians; but their courage, Sherwood felt at the time, was quite probably meaningless, gestural, and tragically comic.[18]

Sherwood was by no means alone in his fixation on characters caught in the breech between dead religion and dangerous science. The depiction of this kind of dislocated person was a major theme in the plays, films, and novels of the depression. Outstanding examples of this type are the "romantic" ballerina and jewel thief in Vicki Baum's *Grand Hotel* (1930); the silent-screen stars in Kaufman and Hart's *Once in a Lifetime* (1930) and the old actors in Kaufman and Ferber's *Dinner at Eight* (1932); the old and aristocratic judge who kills the dictator and then himself in Rice's melodrama *Judgment Day* (1934); the aristocrat-turned-Nazi who kills himself rather than continue as one of the beasts in Odets's *Till the Day I Die* (1935); the old, "pioneer" grandmother who decries the amorality of the present generation in S. N. Behrman's *End of Summer* (1936); the Grand Duchess, Kolenkhov, and most of the Vanderhoff family in Kaufman and Hart's *You Can't Take It with You* (1936) (Figure 3); Birdie, as the representative of a more gracious past, in Lillian Hellman's *The Little Foxes* (1939); Kit Carson, the

Figure 2. Robert E. Sherwood's "escape mechanism" in action: Lynn Fontanne and Alfred Lunt in *Reunion in Vienna* (1931). (New York Public Library)

fantastic old cowboy who kills the symbolic fascist in Saroyan's *The Time of Your Life* (1939); and the aging aunts, representative of a bygone, small-town Brooklyn, in Joseph Kesselring's *Arsenic and Old Lace* (1941).

Although a few of these characters (like Kit Carson or Grandpa Vanderhoff) experience at least a temporary (and sentimental) triumph, most are forced by the powers of the new age either to die or to experience a symbolic death (like the Brewster sisters being placed in the asylum or Birdie beaten into silence). The best fate that any of the characters meets is that of living life within the confines of a special world detached from the rest of culture. The Vanderhoff residence and Saroyan's bar, examples of these oases from the brutality of change, exist as enchanted circles with their own rules of behavior; but their existence is tenuous and insecure. In both plays, an invader threatens to overthrow the artificial order and is repulsed only after a struggle. In what must have been an attractive fantasy for people of the period who identified with them, these "survivals" ride out their grotesque position but inside a fragile bubble.

The "survival" type seemed to have a special affinity for the theatre (perhaps because it is a "survival" itself), but the figure appeared frequently in the fiction and film of the depression as well. In addition to the superfluous persons of the Old South in *Gone with the Wind,* there were the Joads and other "Okies" of Steinbeck's *The Grapes of Wrath* (1939), driven from their land and their way of life by the relentless encroachment of the bulldozer. These two novels, among the most-read (or, at least, most-purchased) books of the 1930s, also enjoyed enormous popular success as movies. The film versions of *Gone with the Wind* and *The Grapes of Wrath* stood among those made from the plays described above – like *Grand Hotel* (1932), *Dinner at*

Figure 3. An enchanted circle of survivals: the Vanderhoff household and guests in Kaufman and Hart's *You Can't Take It with You* (1936). (New York Public Library)

Eight (1932) and *The Petrified Forest* (1935) – in featuring dislocated characters in narratives of wandering and the search for
a place in an ill-defined new order.[19]

Homogeneity and Hollywood

American film of the depression was no minor entertainment.
After balancing ticket-sales figures with polling data from the
same year, Arthur Schlesinger, Jr., found that in 1937, 61%
of the population went to the movies at least once per week.[20]
Movies became an "industry" in the 1930s, a term still spoken
piously by presenters of Academy Awards, and industrializa-
tion imposed distinct pressures as films, more than ever before,
became products of a business empire. The elements of mystification in the book *Gone with the Wind*, for example, were preserved and exploited in the film version, and such sentimental-
ization was typical of mainstream Hollywood cinema. The film
carried on the cultural "work" of the best-selling novel: building up a heroic image of the American struggling in a desperate social situation and offering a sentimentalized "old days"
as a haven in which to collect one's resources and plan for the
future.

In the case of texts that were not already thoroughly palatable, in that they contained elements of the grotesque, the film
industry was adroit at adaptation. During this process, any disruptive elements were trimmed from the source and the work
was converted into a digestible product of mass consumption.
The conversion of Sherwood's *Idiot's Delight* from disturbing
stage play to screen pabulum (see Chapter 2) can serve as typical, though its transformation from grotesque work to mass-
culture product appears a modest alteration in the face of cer-

tain others. Nathanael West's *Miss Lonelyhearts* (1933), a bitter and grotesque novel about a half-mad and alcoholic columnist spinning through an absurd and nightmarish world to a ridiculous death, was converted into a comedy (*Advice to the Lovelorn*, 1933) starring Lee Tracy as a wisecracking columnist who builds his column into a business empire. Lillian Hellman's *The Children's Hour* (1934) was translated onto film as a conventional, heterosexual love triangle (*These Three*, 1936) starring Merle Oberon and Joel McCrea. Countless other examples illustrate the same process of homogenization and highlight the significant difference between Hollywood cinema of the depression (as an institution that consumed texts and then regurgitated them for a hungry public) and contemporaneous theatre and fiction (which retained – to a limited degree – the ability to express disruptive ideologies).

In recent decades, Broadway productions have increasingly become products for a national audience of tourists, and rising production costs have made the business more conservative and dependent on proven formulas that display exactly the "part-interchangeability" that Adorno attributes to products of any "culture industry." Depression-era theatre, on the other hand, was still a relatively localized institution in which artists had significant responsibility for the way their work was presented. Theatre in the 1930s was consequently less a part of the industry of mass culture and less subject to its pressures to homogenize and narcotize. This is not to say that the theatre was somehow free from pressure to conform to the dominant ideology; even a cursory analysis of any season from the period shows that this was not the case. It was, rather, a situation in which the theatre was freer to introduce disruptions than was the highly efficient and top-directed machine of Hollywood.

A similar comparison could be made between film and fiction in the depression. Publishing was then the province not of a handful of mammoth corporations but of a world of smaller publishing "houses" (a term suggesting a domestic personality for these publishers that makes little sense in the corporate scene of today) usually owned and directed by two or three individuals. These institutions were still, of course, part of a commercial structure and interested in selling books; but localization and the personal involvement of the owner with the product allowed the greater possibility of grotesque and otherwise disruptive works being published. Thus, although Hal Smith of Cape and Smith coached Faulkner into rewriting *Sanctuary* to make it less graphic in its violence and sexual content, the book remains shocking and grotesque. Smith agreed with Faulkner that these were the very qualities that would make the book sell. Both writer and publisher were rewarded when *Sanctuary* became Faulkner's only best-seller.[21]

Horror Films

In spite of the homogenizing power of the Hollywood film industry, grotesque elements thrived in certain corners of its domain during the depression. The massive demand for movies contributed to the burgeoning of a huge variety of low-budget films, allowing some talented but unorthodox directors and designers an exciting and relatively free outlet for their creativity. By far the most experimental and popular genre of low-budget depression films was the new wave of horror pictures that flickered across screens for countless weeknight showings and Saturday matinees.

The horror film had been pioneered in the silent era, but the depression witnessed its maturation into the essential and profitable genre it still remains in American cinema. At the same time, the makers of these films invented the film language for the genre, images and types that – though they today strike us as clichés and are the subject of endless camp – carried a vitality and originality for viewers of the 1930s. Because of the freedom of the horror film to mingle "realism" with fantastic invention and dark humor, it was able to take on the special role of the graphic portrayer of the fears of its mass audience in its own eerie and grotesque vocabulary. In this way, the horror film showed the nation its nightmares about the depersonalizing action of technology, the death of belief, the rise of dictators, and the loss of a clear identity in a narrative language of mad scientists, unwilling transformations, and disfigured faces.

The mad scientist was not invented by the filmmakers of the depression. Its roots go at least as deep as Faustian legend, and the figure is prominent not only in the work of Marlowe and Goethe but also in that of E. T. A. Hoffman, Mary Shelley, Robert Louis Stevenson, Edgar Allan Poe, and Henry James. In film, the type was featured as early as the nineteenth-century experiments of Georges Méliès, and the visual language for the scientist's trickery (in the luring and entrapment of "subjects" for his mad experiments) and transformations was developed in such silents as Fritz Lang's *Metropolis* (1926), in which the benevolent Maria is transformed into an evil and strangely sensual robot.

The depression-era mad scientist of American film, like representations of this mythic figure throughout its history, gave form to the audience's distrust of science's promises of personal and social manipulation and "improvement." This distrust was especially keen in the depression, as science and technology were offered as substitutes for a more familiar way of life that was disappearing. The scientist had emerged during the late twenties as the omnipresent "expert" who offered instruction on carrying out every aspect of modern life, from farming and the breeding of livestock to sexual technique and toilet training. Portrayals of the scientist as a benevolent force were rare in the period – the 1936 film of H. G. Wells's *Things to Come* being the one outstanding example. Instead, the typical screen scientist of the depression was a wild-eyed and evil man, usually insane due to his torment over some injustice done him by society and bent on performing an evil transformation on unwitting or manacled victims. Significantly, the mad scientist – in light of his traumatic past – represents a force for good that was somehow subverted. This motion resonates with the cultural criticism of Sherwood and others who saw the "bright promise" of science in the eighteenth and nineteenth centuries turn out in its full bloom to offer, as its primary gifts, the destructive power of modern warfare and the dehumanization of culture through technology.

In many ways, the prototypical portrayal of the mad scientist in depression film was James Whale's *Frankenstein* (1931), loosely drawn from Mary Shelley's novel of 1818.[22] Baron Henry Frankenstein (Victor in the book) revels in his usurpation of the creative role that culture had traditionally assigned to God. He creates the Monster not as a free creature but as an object, his personal property over which he wants complete sovereignty. His laboratory is not a place of enlightenment and discovery but a forbidden chamber, filled with bubbling tubes and the frightening and seemingly random charges of screaming current passing between electrodes. In spite of his empty declarations of humanitarian purpose, Baron Frankenstein is the scientist bent on his own neurotic purpose, which he disguises behind the rhetoric of "progress." He is in love with his own power and indifferent to the safety or welfare of his creation or the rest of humankind.

The mad scientist figure is doubled in Whale's sequel, *Bride of Frankenstein* (1935), with the addition of the evil Dr. Pretorious, who forces Frankenstein to create the bride as a mate for the Monster and so allow the procreation of a whole race of monsters – a theme with clear resonance with the Nazis' "scientific" aspirations toward genetic manipulation. The resonance with the growing threat of Nazi Germany was also unmistakable in Whale's other horror classic of the depression, adapted from an H. G. Wells novel: *The Invisible Man* (1933). Here, the damaged scientist grows increasingly insane and violent and – in rhetoric reminiscent of Hitler's in the same year – vows to pillage and terrorize the entire world.

The theme of malevolent manipulation of people by the scientist was also taken up in a film adaptation of Wells's *The Island of Dr. Moreau.* In Eric Kenton's *Island of Lost Souls* (1933), Dr. Moreau has transformed hundreds of animals into quasi-humans, the most successful specimen being a panther-woman. Moreau is a sadistic and insane dictator on his island, torturing his creatures in the "House of Pain" and seeking a kind of godhood in mating the panther-woman with a marooned sailor.

Victor Halperin's *White Zombie* (1932) links the mad scientist with the power of voodoo in the figure of the plantation owner (Bela Lugosi) who, by the use of drugs and magic, controls hordes of workers who slave as zombies on his sugar plantation. The mechanical movements of the zombies seem to refer at times to newsreel images of ranks of goose-stepping Nazis (elevated to a hideous beauty in Leni Riefenstahl's 1935 *Triumph of the Will*) and at other times to films of Soviet youths performing mass calisthenics. The theme of control over the unwilling was also developed in such films as Archie Mayo's *Svengali* (1931, based on Du Maurier's 1894 *Trilby*) and Karl Freund's *Mad Love* (1935), the latter offering the peculiar psychological problem of a man whose transplanted hands have the habit of acting beyond his control.

Related to these narratives of innocents under the control of insane and charismatic figures is the myth of the vampire and its depiction in depression film. The visual language for the myth was initiated by silent treatments, the prime example being F. W. Murnau's *Nosferatu* (1922), based on Bram Stoker's book *Dracula;* but the myth reached a truly mass public in the United States for the first time in the film *Dracula* (1931), directed by Tod Browning and starring Bela Lugosi (who had played the role both on Broadway in 1927 and in a subsequent national tour). The film caused a minor sensation and was followed by a sequel, *Dracula's Daughter* (1936), directed by Lambert Hillyer.

The vampire myth carried special power for Americans in the 1930s in that it combined the images of evil control over innocents (the vampire has a hypnotic gaze) with the insidious transformation of the unwilling. Dracula exercises control over the ravaged mind of Renfield and engages in a battle of wills with Dr. Van Helsing for control of the young Lucy Harker. In *Dracula's Daughter*, the female vampire – an artist who tries to be "cured" of her vampirism by a doctor but finds her story rejected as ridiculous – seduces a young model through mind control and then drains the woman of her blood. Both films rely for their effect on the anxiety of being turned into something against one's will.

Besides the Dracula pictures, this kind of transformation is also central to the narratives of *Dr. Jekyll and Mr. Hyde* (1932), a film that also plays on the figure of the mad scientist;[23] *The Werewolf of London* (1935); *The Wolf Man* (1941); and Jacques Tourneur's *Cat People* (1942). In each of these films, people are transformed either as the result of mad science (as in *Dr. Jekyll and Mr. Hyde*) or a biologically transmitted curse (as in *Cat People* and the werewolf films). Once transformed they perform acts that they would never consider in their "normal" state, and the narratives take on a tragic quality as the characters are unable to escape from the compulsion to injure and kill. They search for a cure through science, but its representatives are blinded by their own egoism and offer no help. The pathetic heroine of *Cat People* – sensing that if she has sex with her husband she will turn into a giant cat and kill him – is sent by him to a psychiatrist. A good Freudian, he assures her that she is simply the victim of sexual anxiety and neurosis.

A special kind of transformation occurs in the many films of the period that involve the shrinking or miniaturization of people. Dr. Pretorious has a collection of shrunken humans in *Bride of Frankenstein,* and this kind of transformation forms the basis for Tod Browning's unsettling *The Devil Doll* (1936). In this film, cowritten by Eric von Stroheim, a man who was sent to Devil's Island as the result of a frame-up reduces people to the size of dolls and forces them to enact his revenge on those who framed him. A similar effect is used in Ernest Schoedsack's *Dr. Cyclops* (1940), the story of a mad scientist who shrinks people who become suspicious about his experiments.

These narratives of mad scientists, mind control, vampirism, forced transformation, and the diminution of human beings – occurring as they did within one genre and within one decade – are cultural signs of the grotesque (Figure 4). They stand as depictions of the culture's anxiety at being transformed, seemingly against its will, into a destructive and insensible monster by a scientific cult that it hardly trusted. Longing to be "cured" and to return to "normalcy," Americans were finding the way blocked, the foundations of religion and commerce having crumbled behind them. They were left to wander in the world as monsters or as miniatures, transformed, confused, diminished.

In spite of the homogenizing power of the Hollywood industry from which they issued, these films remained ideologically disruptive. The victims of the transformations do not find cures, and the evil that is the source of tension in the narrative is not, in most cases, permanently defeated. In formal terms, the films tend to break the rules of "easy" narratives (invisible editing, timed reaction shots, unintrusive articulations) and exploit techniques that call attention to themselves, such as extreme angles, long takes, or temporal and spatial ellipses.

The films are also disruptive in the grotesque images that they present: a monster playing with a child, a man kissing a creature who is half woman and half panther, a young woman purring and crouching like a cat in heat, people reduced to the size of rodents and darting like rats among middle-class furnishings. These images, the result of a conflation of disparate things, defy facile categorization or dismissal. As a result, they are devoid of any narcotizing effect and operate as a thorn in the side of an industry that relies heavily on sentiment to supply "satisfying" conclusions. Still, because of the peripheral position of the horror films in the studio structure and because of the special allowances that culture has always extended toward the horror genre (it seems to answer so powerful a psychological demand that it escapes conventional moral judgments), these films were released and received wide distribution. The limit of the culture industry's tolerance of this attack from

Figure 4. The fear of unwilling transformation: Bela Lugosi's hypnotic gaze in a publicity still for the film *Dracula* (1931).

within was demonstrated, however, in the suppression of the most disruptive American motion picture of the depression: Tod Browning's notorious exhibition of human deformity, *Freaks*.[24]

Film Farce

The early thirties saw the rise of a species of hard-edged, antisentimental farce in the films of the Marx Bros., W. C. Fields, and Mae West. Joanna Rapf has called these films "amoralfarces" and noted their connection with the comic pieces of other periods of economic and social collapse.[25] These films are "amoral" in that they are animated by pure aggression that is not "backed up by the conviction of right" but instead is "enjoying itself without reference to the moral issues which may be involved" (p. 190). The amoral stance of these farces carries with it an inherent destructiveness and overturning of conventions; Rapf describes the genre as depicting "a topsy-turvy world delighting in its own anarchy" (p. 192).

The four films released by the Marx Bros. between 1930 and 1933 are vivid illustrations of the power of the grotesque to deflate established institutions, a power that Bakhtin observed in the folk festivals of medieval Europe. The films take on aspects of the grotesque when nonsensical language or illogical actions are extreme enough to assume a double quality of hilarity and menace. The nonsensical exchanges between Groucho Marx and Louis Sorin in Victor Heerman's *Animal Crackers* (1930), based on the 1928 Kaufman–Ryskind stage play, are funny and threatening, as conventions of language and meaning break down and the order of communication is overturned. In Leo McCarey's *Duck Soup* (1933), both the narrative – with

Groucho as a ridiculously incompetent national leader who is praised as a hero – and specific physical "bits" – such as Harpo washing his feet in the vendor's lemonade – produce a fictional world that is far from safe.

The release of *Animal Crackers* and Norman McLeod's *Monkey Business* (1931) in France caught the attention of Antonin Artaud and led him to a definition of the films as "surreal" instruments of liberation and "deliverance."[26] Although Artaud did not use the word "grotesque," the conflation and doubleness that he describes in the Marx Bros. films provide a lucid description of a grotesque farce. In order to understand the "absolute originality" of these two films, writes Artaud,

. . . one would have to add to the notion of humor the notion of something disturbing and tragic, a fatality . . . which slips in behind it, like the revelation of a dreadful illness on a profile of absolute beauty. . . . If the Americans, to whose spirit this genre of film belongs, refuse to see these films as anything but humorous, and if they insist on limiting themselves to the superficial and comical connotations of the word "humor," so much the worse for them, but this will not prevent us from regarding the finale of *Monkey Business* as a hymn to anarchy and total rebellion. . . . And the triumph of all this is in the kind of exaltation, both visual and auditory, that all these events acquire in the half light, in the degree of vibration they achieve and in the kind of powerful disturbance that their total effect ultimately produces in the mind. (pp. 240–2)

The "powerful disturbance" that Artaud distinguishes in the early Marx Bros. films effects a social as well as a personal liberation as the grotesque shatters conventional patterns of hierarchy and submission. This destructive action, which will also be found in *Hellzapoppin* and other "outrageous" theatre pieces of the depression, is described by Susan Stewart in her structuralist study of nonsense. She explains the connection between the anarchical work of art and a disruption of metonymy that extends to the social sphere:

While all language assumes a possible society, while all language is utopian, all nonsense divides and rearranges any idea of society as coherent and integral. Nonsense threatens the disintegration of an infinite 'making conscious,' an infinite movement of undercutting the world all at once and over and over again. It refuses the uplifting note by which the world assumes a happy ending.[27]

If the Marx Bros. added threat to humor by resorting to nonsense and anarchy, W. C. Fields achieved a similar effect by the direct contradiction of conventional expectations for "moral" behavior. In all of his films throughout the depression, he plays the role of an antihero, a loafing, lying, often cruel character who nevertheless retains an uneasy sympathy on the part of the viewer. We are given the chance to take pleasure in the puncturing of the usual codes of "good" behavior as well as the conventional aspirations of bourgeois America. Fields presents a subversive attack on the mythos symbolized by Horatio Alger, as he portrays a likable ne'er-do-well who avoids absolutely the hard work and honesty that the Alger myth advocates and yet is rewarded in the end through a twist of "dumb luck."

Fields's threat to the institutions that order the life of his audience found a parallel in the depression films of Mae West; but where Fields threatened the American virtues of hard work and honesty, West attacked conventional attitudes toward sex. In all of her films of the depression – *She Done Him Wrong* (1933), *I'm No Angel* (1933), *Belle of the Nineties* (1934), *Goin' to Town* (1934), *Klondike Annie* (1936), *Go West Young Man* (1936), *Every Day's a Holiday* (1938), *My Little Chickadee* (1940) – she overturned conventional notions of what women wanted in life and of how they could go about getting it. Bulging out of her tight garments, leering, raising an eyebrow, engaging in sexual double entendres that pressed the tolerance of the industry to its limits, West was at once both comic and threatening, both attacking and titillating American middle-class culture.

The grotesque conflation of comedy with threat was also found in the comic genre that was invented in the "screwball comedies" that arose during the thirties. These films, often traced by historians to the surprise success of Frank Capra's *It Happened One Night* (1934), differed from earlier comedies in that extreme comic situations – including nonsensical exchanges and slapstick humor – were not the realm of secondary characters but were incorporated into the main "romantic" narrative of a pair of antagonists who eventually become lovers. As a genre, these films tend to be less extreme in the level of threat than the farces just examined; but when their narratives do venture into grotesque territory the effect is shocking because the moment comes as a surprise in the context of romantic comedy.

Other Genres

The grotesque was built from different materials in another film genre that matured and commanded great popularity in the depression – the "hard" crime or gangster film. The pattern for these grotesque moments was laid in Mervyn LeRoy's *Little Caesar* (1931), often seen as the progenitor of the gangster film. LeRoy developed a film that mixed extreme violence, an antihero, and sardonic humor in a package that held a strong fascination for the American public. Edward G. Robinson's character (Enrico Bandello) is a sort of Richard III in a modern urban setting: ugly, greedy, cruel, and scheming, he defeats his opponents and gains power, only to be killed in a ridiculous circumstance – not calling for a horse, but gunned down behind a sign for a movie musical called *Tipsy, Topsy, Turvy.* Like Shakespeare's character, Rico provokes an ambivalent response from the audience, as we are both fascinated and repulsed by his ambition and cruelty.

Grotesque elements entered other films of the depression in such an array and in such brief flashes that they resist categorization. The fanciful sometimes turns to the hideous in fantasy films like *Babes in Toyland / March of the Wooden Soldiers* (Meins and Rogers, 1934) or *The Wizard of Oz* (Victor Fleming, 1939). Animated films such as Disney's *Snow White and the Seven Dwarfs* (1938) and *Pinocchio* (1940) contain both images and story elements that border on the horrific. *King Kong* (Cooper and Schoedsack, 1933) and MGM's Tarzan series (1932–41) draw on the threat of a savagery that is always on the verge of being unleashed. What is consistent in all of these films is that the presence of the grotesque is directly related to whatever disruptive effect the film might have. As such, the grotesque proves itself to be – in popular entertainment just as in high art – the enemy of aesthetic narcotization.

The Hays Code

What remains to be considered is the reaction of the culture industry to this widespread challenge. In the case of cinema, the reaction took the form of the Production Code. Under pressure from the Legion of Decency and from conservative politicians, the Motion Picture Producers and Distributors of America created the code in 1930 and enforced it beginning in 1934. The code did not limit itself to defining specific words or actions that could not be presented, but took in a much broader scope that sought to "reform" American film in every element of narrative, and so ideological, language. The code held as a general principle that "no picture shall be produced which will lower the standards of those who see it. . . . Hence the sympathy of the audience should never be thrown to the side of crime, wrongdoing, evil or sin."[28] The code insisted that films must build the "right ideals" and inculcate the "right principles" in their audiences. The specific rules included requirements that "methods of crime shall not be explicitly presented" and that "the sanctity of the institution of marriage and the home shall be upheld." "Excessive and lustful kissing, lustful embracing, suggestive postures and gestures" were not to be shown, and in the area of violence, "actual hangings or electrocutions . . . brutality and possibly gruesomeness" were to be "treated within the careful limits of good taste." The intent of the code was, it seems in retrospect, not simply to protect the "morals" of the population but to harness the disruptive power of the medium and so protect the status quo. The disruptive elements of the grotesque, which often consisted of threats to conventional order and sexual mores, were thus severely limited. Artists like the Marx Bros., their threatening edge removed, settled into banal and predictable films in the latter half of the thirties, a period that saw the rise of a wave of sentimental comedies directed by Frank Capra. Fields and West fared better under the code because they relied more on implication and innuendo and less upon direct assault. The screwball comedies and later gangster films managed to redeem themselves sufficiently by steering clear of "hard-core" sexual content and providing conventionally moral conclusions worthy of George Lillo. Still, one must consider the code to have been effective in its controlling action when one considers the general turn that American cinema took at the time of its enforcement – a turn away from a disruptive expression of sex, anarchy, and violence and toward a type of product that buttressed patriarchal capitalism through a blithe mixture of sentiment, amusement, and happy endings.

Theatre and Complexity

At first, it is hard to know where to begin in considering the place of the theatre in this matrix of cultural collision and grotesque expression in depression America. Not only was the sheer volume of production quite large – as the Little Theatre movement continued to bear fruit across the country and the Federal Theatre Project added a whole new class of professional productions – but in addition the ambivalent nature of the grotesque itself makes the phenomenon difficult to recognize.

Once identified, the grotesque presents another problem: It appears as a thread connecting a list of productions that have little or no formal resemblance to one another; hence, one is hard-pressed to argue that this odd collection really display the same "thing." Does the hideous and comic characterization of the Queen of Hearts in so "innocent" a production as Eva Le Gallienne's *Alice in Wonderland,* for example, really lead to the same aesthetic experience as the horrific, hysterically pitched torture scene in John Howard Lawson's *Marching Song*? Both plays seem to contain multiple examples of the grotesque, but *Alice in Wonderland* attracted many thousands of playgoers (enough to sustain Le Gallienne's struggling company for almost a year) whereas *Marching Song* was unpopular enough to prompt the final collapse of the Theatre Union, which had invested heavily in the elaborate set and enormous cast. Clearly, the grotesque was only one element in a complex theatrical package and no guarantor of public interest or financial success.

The key to the question of why some grotesque theatre proved useful to culture (and so attracted a large audience) while other examples were largely ignored is the factor of cultural *resonance*. In certain productions the complex of signs that constitute a piece of theatre (play, performers, location, scene, advertising, mythology of rumors and gossip, ticket price, and so on) resonated with its cultural frame, and thus the production attracted a large audience.[29] Within that group of "resonant" productions are many that were essentially grotesque, and I see these as falling into one of three categories, each reflecting a different *use* of the grotesque. In defining these three categories, I do not mean to impose an artificial taxonomy but to identify "connection points" in the cultural structure: points at which specific works of art connected with the cultural frame of ideology and social psychology. These categories cannot automatically be applied to other periods, since they stem from the specific cultural moment of the United States during 1930–41. As I see the grotesque theatre of the period and its surrounding cultural frame, the three points of connection are the following: the analogy of mixed form, the burlesque of anxiety, and chaos in the theatrical space.

2

The Political Analogy
Or, "Tragicomedy" in an In-Between Age

No generation that has ever lived has seen as much history being made as has mine. Born in the last years of Victoria, with
limitless security in prospect – and then, all of human life
completely disrupted by emancipation of women, great war,
automobiles, airplanes, radio, Communism, Fascism, prohibition, Freud, movies, economic collapse. And the result so far?
Emphatic improvement.
> – from Robert E. Sherwood's diary, 1937.[1]

IS NOTHING NEW to point out that "tragicomedy" –
erm that dates from Plautus – has come into special
minence in the twentieth century. The word has a flex-
ibi at allows a cutting across the four genres – tragedy,
con melodrama, farce – four words that are perfectly ade-
qua he job of describing the formal characteristics of al-
mo arrative. However, I shall adapt a strategy from the
criti sopher Susanne Langer and distinguish between
"lite m" and "feeling form," and so use the word "tragi-
com get at elements that provoke a conflicted *feeling* in

audiences rather than to describe a particular set of formal characteristics. I do not mean, for example, that all of the depression plays described here begin as tragedies and end as comedies; nor do they necessarily follow a reverse order. In terms of their formal characteristics, many of these plays, so complex in their dramatic contracts with audiences, are "comedies." Others are "melodramas." Others would likely require hyphenation to describe them formally, as in the case of one prominent "farce-melodrama." What they have in common is a heavily loaded dramatic contract, one in which "clauses" inviting comic and tragic responses alternate serially, prompting us at one moment to objectivity and laughter and at the next moment to empathy and profound sad feeling; or in which the "clauses" are written multiply, on top of one another and having an equal or near-equal weight, producing that suspenseful, odd, grotesque response of neither-happy-nor-sad, a twist, a painful wringing.

In a well-known 1927 essay in praise of Conrad's *The Secret Agent,* Thomas Mann found this breaking down of traditional categories to be "the striking feature of modern art . . . with the result that the grotesque is its most genuine style."[2] Mann statement is verified easily enough in our thinking about theatre by a glance around a century that includes the world playwrights like Anton Chekhov, Luigi Pirandello, Max Fri Friedrich Dürrenmatt, Samuel Beckett, Joe Orton, Ha Pinter, Caryl Churchill, David Rabe, Sam Shepard, and I Mamet. All of these writers, to name only a few of the prominent, have dealt extensively in the deliberate mix comic and serious content and situations, or the treatm horrific material in a comic context in such a way that t matic contract with the audience is fraught with amb and unrelieved tension.[3] These plays are produced i professional and university theatres and are widely read by students in survey courses. In short, we have come to see this mixed aesthetic as a normal thing.

What theatre specialists have gotten used to, however, is hardly an accurate barometer of popular taste. As much as the theatre still exists as a popular form – and such a case can be made if one counts the thousands of performances put on yearly by amateur groups in high schools and community theatres – the playwrights mentioned above are not essential parts of the repertoire. It is almost impossible, for example, to imagine the Muncie Civic Theatre producing *Sticks and Bones* or even *Waiting for Godot* – a play that has become an icon for intellectuals and academics.[4] Rather, the playwrights named above are all part of an intellectual elite, participants in a "high art" overtly opposed to the dominant ideology, their plays typifying Mann's analysis of tragicomedy as "the genuine anti-bourgeois style" (p. 241). The American purveyors of tragicomedy in the Great Depression were, by contrast, at the very center of the commercial theatre. Plays like *Idiot's Delight* and *Arsenic and Old Lace* were produced profitably in New York, enjoyed successful national tours, were mounted by amateur companies in "little" theatres across the country and – though in softened versions – presented to a mass public through the extended medium of Hollywood cinema. So many of these plays were produced in the "mainstream" commercial theatre, and so successful were they, that they signify a major trend in the popular entertainment of the period.

I do not wish to argue, then, that American culture of the depression was unique in producing tragicomedy, but that this mixed form had a special resonance with the cultural frame of the time, a resonance manifested in the unusual phenomenon of the grotesque being sought after and paid for by bourgeois theatregoers and bourgeois institutions. In my view, this temporary popularity of and demand for so tense and ambivalent a kind of entertainment was the result of the unconscious connection made in the minds of artist and audience alike between this aesthetic form and the cultural moment itself. For many people of that moment, the tragicomic feeling experienced in a theatre served as a satisfying metaphor for the position of their culture: torn between an agricultural past and a technological future, suffering from a sense of dislocation and confusion, threatened by wars that they feared could wipe out civilization as they knew it – all of this encased within and mixed together with an incongruous, hardy optimism. The doubleness and self-contradiction of these comedies gave a form to vague feelings, and the pleasure that people felt in recognizing this "reality" onstage led to their popularity; the plays symbolized in their uneasy form the culture's sense of hanging between possibilities of a glorious technological future and a dehumanizing chaos of social collapse and world war.[5]

To be sure, the popular form taken by American tragicomedy in the thirties did not display the hard edge of the more elitist, intellectually demanding works of the European modernists, like Pirandello or Frisch, nor the naked threat of more recent American models, like Shepard or Mamet. Although American "Broadway" playwrights of the thirties often presented criticism of American social life and culture, they did not set out to overthrow it. These were commercial artists, interested in commercial success, who – in most cases – hoped to present "significant" ideas to a mass audience within the forms they knew best. In this mixture of "theme" and entertainment, an unintentional, commercial grotesque emerged on Broadway. The outstanding exception to this pattern was *Arsenic and Old*

Lace – a play designed entirely for fun and virtually devoid of intellectual content.

Of the 276 plays and musicals that ran for over one hundred performances in New York between 1930 and 1940, 35 contain the essential requirements of self-contradiction and ambivalence in the dramatic contract.[6] In spite of their success in New York, some of the plays – like Lynn Riggs's *Russet Mantle* (1936) or S. N. Behrman's *End of Summer* (1936) – were little seen beyond their Broadway runs. Others, however, were among the most revived pieces (in tours, amateur productions, and in some cases on film) of the decade: *Grand Hotel* (1930), *Brief Moment* (1931), *Reunion in Vienna* (1931), *The Animal Kingdom* (1932), *Dinner at Eight* (1932), *Biography* (1932), *The Petrified Forest* (1935), *High Tor* (1936), *Idiot's Delight* (1936), *Stage Door* (1936), *The Women* (1936), *Rocket to the Moon* (1938), *No Time for Comedy* (1939), *The Time of Your Life* (1939), and *The Male Animal* (1940). These were joined in 1941 by a play that emerged as the most popular – and in some ways, most extreme – example of this genre. *Arsenic and Old Lace* began what was to be a three-year run on Broadway and a career as one of the plays most produced by amateur companies in the United States.

One can get a sense of the cultural work of this thirties style of American tragicomedy, and of the political concerns that animated their narratives, by looking at several pointed examples in plays by Robert E. Sherwood, Clare Boothe Luce, S. N. Behrman, William Saroyan, and Joseph Kesselring.

Robert E. Sherwood

Dürrenmatt has argued that a grotesque form of comedy contains a possibility for precision and objectivity that is wholly foreign to "what the public understands as humour, which is a coziness which is now sentimental and now frivolous."[7] Such plays contain an inherent "cruelty of objectivity," and are thus "capable of assimilating questions of the time and even more the present itself, without being propaganda or journalism." A certain species of depression theatre is described by Dürrenmatt's formulation, with its implications of a conscious construction by the artist of a dissimilar, jarring collection of incidents and of comedy used as a kind of purveyor of a didactic content. Robert E. Sherwood's *Idiot's Delight* was really the epitome of this kind of piece in the 1930s.

The success of Sherwood's plays in the forum of the Theatre Guild and its system of touring houses is a testament not just to the theatregoing public's satisfaction in seeing the grotesque situation of the era given a form, but – more especially here – to the rich "entertainment" value in the comic form. In *Idiot's Delight,* just as he had done the previous year in *The Petrified Forest*, Sherwood presented a dark vision of the historical moment and of the insidious, apparently ageless tendency of humankind toward prejudice and greed. In both cases, however, he managed to leave audiences smiling and – in the case of *Idiot's Delight* – humming a merry tune.

The odd, irresolved quality of Sherwood's depression plays has been an essential criticism of their literary value. At the time of its original production, Brooks Atkinson found the play "a larkish good time," but its discussion of war "inconclusive," the mood of the play being "somewhat too trivial for such a macabre subject."[8] Later in the year, when the play was awarded the Pulitzer Prize, Atkinson wrote a long column gently criticizing the selection and suggesting that Maxwell Anderson's *Winterset* was more deserving. *Idiot's Delight* was, for Atkinson, "a gaudy show" seasoned with "several passionate attacks upon

militaristic nationalism."[9] The slender folder of serious criticism
that has been done on Sherwood since the thirties shows that
later scholarly critics have seen these incongruities as strange,
if not exactly damning. Malcolm Goldstein found that Sherwood "[l]ed on" his audience to expect "a romantic ending"
and then shocked them by blowing up the potential lovers in
their small hotel.[10] C. W. E. Bigsby has written that Sherwood
was offering "the absolution of moral seriousness in plays which
combined sentimental personal drama with portentous allegory."[11] Such a mixture was destined to aesthetic failure, Bigsby
implies, since the plays flirt with a kind of commitment, voiced
by a sympathetic survival character, but the character is not
given the agency to make any difference in his or her world.
The unsustained, "quixotic gestures" of Sherwood's Harry
Van contribute to a play that is "for all its success, riddled
with contradiction and unconscious ambiguity" (p. 143). Brenda Murphy, in her study of the development of American stage
realism, sees Sherwood's earlier work (in particular, his 1927
The Road to Rome) as part of the integration of Shavian discussion into American realism. Murphy describes Sherwood's par-
tial deviation from realism in *Idiot's Delight,* referring to the
"surrealistic juxtaposition" of Irene and Harry's hymn singing
with the sounds of exploding bombs and the bursts of machine
guns.[12] The Shavian comparison seems especially telling, considering the near-parallel endings of *Idiot's Delight* and Shaw's
Heartbreak House (1919), in which the disaffected intellectuals
and romantics of Shaw's metaphorical England call out their
invitations to the bombers to blow up their ship of state.

The response of critics and audiences to *Idiot's Delight* was
no accident but the result of careful aesthetic calculation on the
playwright's part. To present a dark vision within an entertaining Broadway package was exactly Sherwood's intention.

Sherwood is a fascinating example of an artist acutely aware of a personal mission to reflect the "big issues" of his culture in its moment. In fact, he saw himself quite consciously as a sort of sluice through which the diverse currents of the "mentality" of his age could be channeled and then given form in his plays; the anguish that he felt in trying to live up to this awesome social task is a frequent theme in his diaries. His extreme sensitivity to the growing threat of a world war (Brown describes him as "devouring" several newspapers each day) seems to have been a contributing factor in the breakdown he suffered while writing *The Petrified Forest* in 1934.[13]

Sherwood's angst had first manifested itself, at least to public eyes, in the winter of 1931–2, a season that Sherwood later called "the winter of the deepest depression and of the Lindbergh kidnapping . . . the year before Hitler came to power."[14] In that gloomy time, he wrote a long, surprising, wide-ranging preface to his play *Reunion in Vienna*, which was being produced by the Theatre Guild. The play is a farce about a deposed prince, now employed as a taxi driver, who convinces an old flame, the wife of a distinguished Freudian psychologist, to have a one-night sexual fling with him after a pathetic reunion party of former aristocrats now brought low. The roles of the prince and the "modern" wife were specially crafted for the Lunts, and the play ran for over six months, which constituted a relative financial success in one of the worst years in the history of the U.S. economy. The play reads as it was received – as an amusing star vehicle. Readers who paused over the preface of the printed play, however, were probably surprised to find that it contained a dark and pessimistic social thesis. The preface is not so much a theatrical document as it is a piece of unrelievedly grim cultural criticism.

Sherwood began the essay with an analysis of the state of the world, Western intellectual life, and the peripheral place of the theatre in that dreary matrix. *Reunion in Vienna* was an example of the "escape mechanism" in operation (p. vii).[15] There was, he wrote, no more popular mechanism than this one in the present "obstreperously technological period" and no better indication of the "spirit of moral defeatism" that "now prevails" in the West. The historic emergency of the thirties is especially painful, because now the advances in education and media allowed the common person to see his or her true situation: a generation occupying "the limbo-like interlude between one age and another." Looking to the past, they see a "shell-torn No Man's Land, filled with barbed-wire entanglements and stench and uncertainty," while their future shows them only "black doubt." Finding no comfort going forward and certainly none in going back, there is much desperate casting about in search of methods of defense. Tradition offers them religion, but they see it is "a stringless bow, impotent in its obsolescence" (p. viii). Modern thought offers them science, but it is a "boomerang" that proffers horror when it promises salvation. Nothing remains but for modern people to devise their own pitiful defenses. In Europe, desperation has led to the "heroic but anachronistic attempt to recreate the illusions of nationalism," the people "drugging themselves with the comforting hope that tomorrow will be a repetition of yesterday, that the Caesars and Tudors will return." Because America has had no Caesars or Tudors, its chosen weapon of defense against the crisis is a kind of half-hearted cynicism that is increasingly tremulous and shrill. The only alternative is a species of sentimentalism that derives "exquisite anguish" from staring in the face of futility and horror.

Sherwood went on to describe the sad gestation of the age of reason from the eighteenth century to its birth in the twentieth, "for which have remained the excruciating labor pains and the discovery that the child is a monster" (p. x). He finds the story especially depressing in light of the "ascendent optimism" of the previous century, which led nowhere but to war and dissolution (pp. x–xi). "Man is a sick animal," and his chief symptom is "embittered distrust of all the physicians who would attempt to heal him": both the "discredited vicars of God" who urge humankind to perform the impossible task of returning to an age of faith, and the "discredited ideologues of the laboratory," who are scorned because humankind believes that it was the scientists "who got [them] into this mess" (p. xi).

The dissolution of religion and the failure of science had produced "a prospect of unrelieved dreariness" and a world that seemed headed for the "Perfect State"; to live in such a world would require humankind to undergo "a sort of intellectual castration" to relieve them of the power to imagine (p. xiii). This is the prospect that drives the literature of the period, a literature that should provoke amusement in his generation's descendents (if they are descendents and not laboratory products). Unable to contemplate in good faith either the ruined past or the nightmare of the future, humankind has turned in desperation to brash denial. Fraught with anxiety, flailing for help, people embrace with trembling arms the only remaining manifestation of the individualism that first distinguished humans from the animals: the anarchistic impulse, "rigorously inhibited but still alive – the impulse to be drunk and disorderly, to smash laws and ikons, to draw a mustache and beard on the Mona Lisa, to be a hurler of bombs and monkey wrenches – to be an artist and a damned fool" (pp. xiv–xv). All of this sad prognostication was used as preface to *Reunion in Vienna*, the playwright sighed, "because it provides confession of the apprehensions from which, with the help of God and a few Lunts, I have been attempting in this play to escape" (p. xvi).

In his plays of the 1930s, Sherwood transformed into action and character his sense of the dissolution of American culture. The "survival" motif of the 1930s permeates his work, as fossils from the earth's civilized past wander rather desperately through a newly barbaric world. In addition to the prince and the other former aristocrats in *Reunion in Vienna* – ridiculous, comic figures in the context of a "new" Austria – stand the "survivals" who figure prominently in Sherwood's other plays. Alan Squier, the melancholy wanderer in *The Petrified Forest* (1935), describes himself as "part of a vanishing race . . . one of the intellectuals."[16] The "petrified forest" itself is a symbol for the state of the world, its past fossilized and lifeless, its present a wilderness ruled by "apes" like the gangster Duke Mantee (Figure 5). *Idiot's Delight* (1936) presents a world gone mad and on the verge of a world war. The play is peopled largely by survivals – idealists, humanists, well-meaning patriots – who must either "adapt" to the brave new world (as does the scientist who throws off cancer research to build bombs for the Fatherland) or be destroyed, as will most everybody else. The Marxist revolutionary is executed during the course of the play, and the patriotic Mr. Cherry's gruesome battlefield death is foreseen by Irene in a hideous vision.

Though *The Petrified Forest* proved financially successful, and Sherwood had managed to encapsulate in Alan Squier his "message" of the reversion of the world to barbarism, the playwright was not pleased with the result. Just as he had criticized *Reunion in Vienna* (1931) for sacrificing its ideas to its comedy, he saw the intellectual content of *The Petrified Forest* as being too easily detachable from the entertainment vehicle.[17] His remarks to a reporter display a frustration at not being able to mix the two elements in such a way as to make the play more intellectually disturbing:

The trouble with me is that I start with a big message and end up with nothing but good entertainment. Do the great run of theatregoers peel off their banknotes to see an Indian fighter, a gunman, a millionaire and an American Legionnaire symbolizing the passing of a world order? In a pig's eye! They come to see two parts of a highly improbable and sentimentalized romance stirred, like a martini, with one part gun-play. They don't want a message and, anyway, perhaps I didn't give it to them as I should have.[18]

He was far more satisfied with *Idiot's Delight*, produced the following year. Sherwood called the play "a compound of blank pessimism and desperate optimism, of chaos and jazz"; he felt that he had at last succeeded in creating an undissectable metaphor for the state of the world, a powerful statement inextricably encased in an entertaining package that would attract many listeners.[19] At Lynn Fontanne's suggestion during rehearsals, he added the scene between Irene and Weber – the weapons manufacturer – in which Irene describes a nightmarish vision of the world at war, of the young English couple dead, "the embryo from her womb splattered against the face of a dead bishop."[20] Sherwood felt even better about the play with this new scene, agreeing with the Theatre Guild board that it gave the play an appropriate "weight." As the production date approached, he expressed the urgency of his feelings in graphic terms. It was, he wrote, the best chance he had ever had to "discharge ideas" that had "long been boiling" in his mind and heart: "In fact, this play is like a 100% orgasm."[21]

Figure 5. The beast overthrows an exhausted culture: Humphrey Bogart and Leslie Howard in Sherwood's *The Petrified Forest* (1935). (New York Public Library)

The production of *Idiot's Delight* was an impressive social document of the years 1935–6 and in its symbolic resonance forms a kind of theatrical model of an American view of Western culture in that moment. Besides the amalgam of themes that appear in the text of the play, the mixture of violent events from the headlines with scenes of light comedy and even musical revue, the array of characters that can be read as allegorical figures for their respective cultures, and the uncanny prediction of border incidents that would provoke the inevitable outbreak of world war, the physical environment itself carried symbolic power. Irene says that this hotel lobby conveys "an amusing kind of horror," and Lee Simonson's set – designed in consultation with Sherwood – gave physical form to the vague sense of dislocation that was typical of the 1930s.

The set was designed as a virtual parody of the Modern design that had come to appear in every part of American life (Figure 6). Simonson himself was well-known outside of theatrical circles as a designer of furniture and utensils in the new, "streamlined" style of sweeping curves and parallel decorative lines, part of the thirties' sense of having to start over from scratch since decorative themes from the past were irrelevant in an age of technology.[22] The combination of the curved walls of the set with the overworked repetition of the parallel horizontal brass strips that line them pushes these characteristic motifs almost to the level of a joke. The most striking object in the room was the piano – a white art deco monstrosity of efficient angularity. It was on this ridiculous instrument that Irene and Harry belted out their salvation as the bombs crashed about them in the play's final moment.

The theatrical elements of that final image formed for Sherwood a complex sign for the grotesque condition of Western civilization in 1936: Harry and Irene are situated in this artifi-

Figure 6. "An amusing kind of horror": Fontanne and Lunt on Lee Simonson's "stream-lined" set in Sherwood's *Idiot's Delight* (1936). (New York Public Library)

cial and meaningless environment, a place stripped of any reference to the past in an attempt to project a machinelike efficiency. Seated at an instrument that is the apotheosis of this absurd lack of history, they belt out "Onward Christian Soldiers" in a ridiculous, desperate, comic invocation of a tradition with which they have no connection, and in absurd, comic defiance of the bombs that rain down outside, threatening to blow the whole confused and artificial mess into bits of curving rubble.

The sign becomes richer if we pull back from the stage image and take in its theatrical frame as well. *Idiot's Delight* was produced by the Theatre Guild, which – by 1936, with its relatively high ticket prices and its extensive system of subscribers nationwide – had become synonymous with a palatable sort of "intellectual" theatre produced in impeccably "good taste." The aggressive screening and tuning of productions by the Guild's board of directors and their arrangement of plays on a "menu" system, offering their subscribers "a taste of this and a slice of that each season," fulfilled with remarkable accuracy Brecht's definition of a "culinary theatre."[23] It was this utterly "aesthetic" approach to theatre, the Guild's detachment from its culture's immediate social concerns, that had led the young Harold Clurman to rebel against his employer and start the Group Theatre. The Guild's commitment to putting on "the best drama of one's time, drama honestly reflecting the author's vision of life or sense of style and beauty" was not enough for idealists of Clurman's generation.[24] Clurman described the Guild in *The Fervent Years* as "put[ting] on plays the way lists of guests were drawn up for parties." (p. 21). The Guild's board "didn't want to say anything through plays, and plays said nothing to them, except that they were amusing in a graceful way, or, if they were tragic plays, that they were 'art' . . . [a]nd art was a good thing" (p. 27). The productions, according to Clurman, were "pretty," and produced in a tone that

was almost always undifferentiatedly correct or standard, according to the nearly latest models, because back of it was no individual drive, only a dilettante acceptance of something someone else – eminently worthy – had first created.[25]

The production of *Idiot's Delight* starred the Lunts – the reigning heroes of the self-conscious "art" theatre of the 1930s – and was also "conceived and supervised" by them.[26] To complete the picture of a production dear to the heart of the "tasteful" bourgeois audience, one should also note that the play was awarded the Pulitzer Prize for 1936.

My point here is to emphasize that *Idiot's Delight* and these other tragicomedic plays of the commercial theatre were not obstreperously "disruptive" in the sense of the Frankfurt School. The effects of these plays were more modest, producing confirmation for the audience members that, yes, the world is in an absurd and perilous state, but leaving them free to conclude their thoughts with, "Now let's go out for a bite!" The Theatre Guild was not the kind of "art" theatre that Adorno envisions as the natural enemy of the "bourgeois ego." The Guild's notion of "art," a notion born of the union of the bohemian roots of the organization with the patrician backgrounds (or at least aspirations) of its board, did not include the need to indict the way of life of the Guild's subscribers. Theatre Guild opening nights were a fabled frenzy of tuxedos and fur coats out for a fine but refined evening of "art" typically followed by an expensive late supper. If the Guild's audience also included less stylish adherents at its matinees and road performances in places like Pittsburgh, Cleveland, and Cincinnati, the theatre's menu nevertheless appealed to people seeking an "intelligent" sort of amusement and – considering the production's comparatively long New York run of 120 performances (in a year when the average run for a straight play was 71) – Sherwood's play was more than sufficient for this purpose.[27] In his history of the Guild, Roy Waldau described the Guild's 1935–6 season as being "obviously one of the more satisfying it had yet offered its subscribers." The Guild enjoyed in 1935 a national subscription list of about fifty thousand hardy souls.[28]

Idiot's Delight, then, was a grotesque play that stood as a theatrical metaphor for its contemporary world, a world it depicted on the verge of obliteration. At the same time, it was produced with impeccable "style" and blessed with the favor of its taste-seeking audience. What does the wholehearted acceptance of such a play in such a milieu mean? It is like the carved images of the "noble grotesque" described by Ruskin. Those gargoyles and impossible creatures stood carved in stone on the public buildings that were the very emblems of "establishment" culture; and – like *Idiot's Delight* – they educated the perceiver, they pointed him or her to a contemplation of the essential issues of life and death, they captured what Ruskin called a "mystery," but they did not offend. The "noble" grotesque is delightful, a thing possessing what Bosanquet calls a "difficult beauty."[29] As an elegant and "tasteful" creation, *Idiot's Delight* was able to circulate within the system, amusing its audience and at the same time providing them an unconscious satisfaction at seeing their nightmare image of the world reified. For some, this collective dream image was rendered a thing of contemplation.

Idiot's Delight was purchased by Metro–Goldwyn–Mayer and released as a film directed by Clarence Brown and starring Norma Shearer and Clark Gable in February of 1939, at a time nearly coincidental with the real war that Sherwood had predicted. The film does preserve some of the play's aesthetic tension between comedy and pathos, but the ending is altered. The "open" ending of Sherwood's play, which operates there as a disruptive element that leads the audience to questions about the role of capitalism in perpetuating war and the possibility of anyone's surviving the next one, is replaced by a "closed" ending that offers a cheap and instant comfort (Figure 7). As in the play, Irene and Harry remain in the lounge to face their fate and belt out tunes as the bombs fall around them, but the film narrative does not end there. Shearer and Gable sing and – in a moment of fear as a bomb lands nearby – they find themselves in close proximity and so have a big kiss. Music swells, and the room grows brighter. The sound of the planes' engines fades. Shearer runs to the window, looks out, turns back to Gable, and says, excitedly, "Oh, Harry, Harry, they've gone! We're going to be all right!" They embrace; music swells again; the screen fades to black.

The ideological work of this Hollywood ending is clear. Whereas the play's ambiguous ending led the audience into questions and discomfort, the film of *Idiot's Delight* offered them a palliative statement that goes something like this: "Yes, war may come, but you will survive and – what's more – love conquers all." The mass-culture industry – unwilling to leave audiences with disturbing questions about war, capitalism, and their own survival in so imminent a conflict – converted the text through a strategy of substitution. The whole motivation of Sherwood's play, to create anxiety in the audience, is thrown out in the film's final moment and replaced by the twin sentimental effects of cheap assurance and instant romance. In the process, the grotesque is erased, a successful product is created, and audiences are properly narcotized.

Sherwood's work in 1938 and after did not require reworking to be made digestible. As the decade progressed and Sherwood joined the Roosevelt administration, his writing became that of a committed activist, the plays elaborately unambiguous. "Survivals" persisted as a character type, but Sherwood began to cast these principled persons in meaningfully heroic roles. Both Lincoln in *Abe Lincoln in Illinois* (1938) and Dr. Valkonen, the Finnish intellectual leader in *There Shall Be No Night* (1940), are presented as martyrs for the ethical traditions of the past. Moreover, their self-sacrifice is no longer meaningless, as it had been in the case of Alan Squier: Sherwood starts writing a world in which things add up, heroism is not an empty word, and self-sacrifice promises, through some system of moral accounting, to yield a better future.

Clare Boothe Luce

Though it was received merely as a burlesque on Hollywood's search for an actress to play Scarlett O'Hara, Clare Boothe Luce's *Kiss the Boys Good-bye* (286 performances, 1938) was intended by her to be a symbolic working out of the easy route fascism could find if it were to rise from the South and charm its way into complete domination of American culture.[30] The play is set in an elegant Connecticut country house that had been converted from its original use as a barn. Into this place of former usefulness but present artificiality come representatives of the dominant culture: the editor of a major New York newspaper, a popular left-wing columnist very much like Heywood Broun, the editor of a magazine very much like the *New Yorker*, a Hollywood producer, an aging movie star, and a studio pitchman. In their selfishness and smart bickering, they

Figure 7. Harry and Irene face the bombers near the end of the Guild production of *Idiot's Delight* (1936). (New York Public Library)

stand for the myopic self-absorption of the bicoastal culture machine, prime and easy pickings for the Southern belle who comes into their midst, manipulates them all through their own selfishness, shoots one of them, knocks them all down – two of them literally – and leaves them admiring her for her aggressiveness. The belle is all subtlety and feigned innocence. She deceives them into believing her to be harmless and stupid and then attacks, her every move cloaked in the trappings of tradition and "plain sense."

Luce used the occasion of the play's publication to blast the stupidity of critics who had not noticed the political subtext of the work. These critics, she wrote, were part of the same cocktail party set of soft-brained intellectuals that were being satirized in the play. As they chattered on, totalitarianism was rising both at home and abroad. It should be noted that Heywood Broun had been the one critic to read the play as political allegory at the time of its opening in October 1938. He published a rollicking satirical review titled, "Kiss the Bourgeoisie Good-Bye," in the *New Republic*. Broun found it hilarious that a woman in Luce's social position wrote a play attacking what he saw as her own set:

Miss Boothe realizes that it is her special mission to bring the light to the bourgeoisie and so she has incorporated her subversive doctrines in a farce fit for the boobs. A hundred years and yet another may pass before a brave new world fully appreciates the sacrifice which Clare Boothe has made for the cause. Indeed, she has made the supreme sacrifice which lies within the capacity of any literary figure. She has compromised her artistic integrity in order to get her message over.[31]

When Luce published her play with its surprising preface in January 1939, a small journalistic war broke out. Harry Hansen of the *New York World-Telegram* wrote a blazing attack on her preface as an absurdity. He had been reading the book in his bed, he cracked wise, and Luce's preface had sent him leaping to the floor to check beneath the bed for Nazis. "A playwright ought to write plays," Hansen wrote, "and let excuses go hang."[32] Heywood Broun then rejoined the fray as the unlikely defender of the playwright. Also writing as a columnist in the *World-Telegram,* Broun endorsed Luce's nomination of the South as the likely source of an American fascist movement. Broun wrote that "fascists are not new in the United States," having posed the main threat to the nation since the time of its founding.[33] The preface itself was then published by the newspaper on 4 February with a note explaining that, in light of the controversy over the preface's assertions about what seemed to most people to be a simple social comedy, the editors had asked Random House for permission to reproduce the preface so that the paper's readers could decide for themselves. The idea was probably just as appealing to Brock Pemberton (the play's producer), considering that the production was still running and the paper's readers might also be tempted to see if they could divine those hidden political messages on their own.

Luce's political allegory was clearer in *Margin for Error* (264 performances, 1939). Here, in the neutral meeting place of an embassy drawing room, representatives of parties vital to the crisis surrounding the rise of Hitler are brought together: the evil Nazi Consul, the good German who eventually will rebel against the Nazis, the stupid and vicious American Bund leader, the likeable Jewish policeman, a "regular" American, two relatives of Nazi victims, and even – through the medium of a blaring radio speech – Adolf Hitler himself. The enactment of the Nazi's death, the policeman's pursuit of the murderer, and the reactions of the participants to the investigation are all part of Luce's metaphor. The "good" people were all driven by necessity to eliminate the Nazi before he could wreak further destruction. He turns out to have inadvertently killed himself by drinking from a poisoned glass he had intended for another.

The preface and press wars continued over the valuation of this play, if not its interpretation. Critics had been quick to note the strange mixtures of the play, and most marveled at the playwright's ability to make farce, melodrama, satire, and politics lie down together. Nearly every critic mentioned this conflation, but Richard Lockridge's review in the *Sun* was the most detailed on the issue. "It takes a murder to bring out the jovial streak in Miss Clare Boothe," he wrote. The central character is murdered "amid hearty chuckles" and "much innocent mirth" is thereby occasioned. Lockridge wrote that "burlesque and melodrama . . . are always uneasy bedfellows" and that now and then in the play "it is difficult to take the murder seriously enough to care about its solution." But Luce overcomes this problem, displaying her ability to "get one in the mood for almost anything."[34]

The main point of contention emerged early in 1940, when the play was published accompanied by a lengthy and rather severely critical preface by – of all people – the playwright's husband, Henry Luce. When the play opened, it was highly touted in certain quarters as the first effective dramatic attack against the Nazis, a play that would somehow laugh the Nazis out of existence (Figure 8). Sidney Whipple, in the *New York World-Telegram,* was especially enthusiastic about the play's power as a political weapon, calling its message "a Dorothy Thompson column as it might have been written by Robert Benchley." Previous anti-Nazi plays had become "bogged down, either in the deadly grimness of the subject or in the sloppy swamp of sentimentality"; but Luce's play was different. Whipple wrote, "Miss Boothe treats the entire ideology of the Reich government as something which, when the world's sense of humor is at last restored, will be laughed to death."[35] Walter Winchell, the most influential "media personality" of the era and a constant fan of Luce's, praised the play in his radio broadcasts and in his columns as the newest weapon in the world's arsenal against the Germans, a farce that was "incessantly caricaturing the Nazis."[36]

Henry Luce was having none of this. His preface to the published play is, among other things, a fourteen-page attack on the notion that theatrical ridicule can defeat a dangerous enemy. Whipple's humor-defeats-the-Nazis theory is "an analysis of the World Crisis which, if correct, might obviously save the British Empire the loss of so much blood and treasure that no time should be lost transmitting it to Mr. Winston Churchill."[37] But the true failing for Henry Luce is not the fault of the play, which does rather well what the theatre is capable of doing. The true failing is the weakness and blindness of the American people, who could so delude themselves as to believe that something as silly as a little play could avert the inevitable military crisis. As the playwright's husband put it:

This preference for a jest, this seeing satire as the only weapon to fight National Socialism – as borne out by the public's relish of *Margin for Error* – proved as clearly as any event in 1939 that the American people either did not dare to say what they meant, or did not wish to have what they said mean anything. It proved not that the American people were honestly confused (for as the self-admittedly best-informed people in history they knew what it was all about) but that they *desired* to be confused, were at great pains to confuse themselves, applaud the confusion, hoped that they might painlessly confuse themselves straight through World War II, and wake up in a fine mood of clarity on some happy summer's day with nothing worse to worry about than the birds twittering too far in advance of the 8:10 Commuter's Special. In short, *Margin for Error* indicated that the United States of America was advancing into its own Munich – a zig-zag isolationist course from which it may or may not extricate itself with honor and success. (p. xi)

Henry Luce's stern lecture to the nation is especially inter-esting in light of the theory of the grotesque. Luce seems to recognize the assistance offered by the grotesque to a popula-tion struggling to cope with overwhelming stress – and he does not like it. Psychological "coping" was not, from Henry Luce's perspective of Presbyterian pragmatism, called for at that or at any time. Such strategies were mere avoidance, softheaded and cowardly. The nation was "informed" about the true situation – in fact, he had spent his entire adult life "informing" them through his publication of *Time, Fortune,* and *Life* magazines – yet the population resorted to this Sherwoodian "escape mechanism" instead of steeling itself to the task and preparing for world war. Ignoring the clearheadedness of Henry R. Luce, the people preferred to fascinate themselves with this artifact that *embodied confusion,* and this son of Presbyterian mission-aries did not like it. It is a pathetic response to the "world-wide challenge to all that we have ever felt about Liberty and Jus-tice and Truth" (p. xix).

Henry Luce was dissatisfied with his wife's clarity of polit-ical purpose and her failure to put forward a character who re-soundingly voiced those capitalized American ideals. In fact, Clare Boothe Luce's plays differ from Sherwood's in her de-liberate manipulation of the conclusion of the narrative to thump her ideological "message." Unlike Sherwood's plays, which tend to end with images of conflict and ambiguity, the metaphor in Luce's comedies is highly specific. In the case of

Figure 8. Killing Hitler, with wit: Otto Preminger confronted by Bramwell Fletcher in Luce's *Margin for Error* (1939). (New York Public Library)

Margin for Error, the ending is unblushingly patriotic, the enactment of a kind of wish-fulfillment regarding the outcome of the war that was about to start. The ideological thread between *Kiss the Boys Good-bye* and *Margin for Error* is clear enough: Luce is arguing the need for "preparedness" and an aggressive response to national threat, a position that she came to represent so vividly in her years as a conservative congresswoman and – later in life – as right-wing saint.[38] Still, her concoctions were too literary for a nuts-and-bolts sort of thinker such as her husband. What Henry Luce seems to want in a play is a democratic-capitalist version of socialist realism in which an unambiguous hero emerges in the drama to voice a straightforward and stirring message that propels the audience from the theatre with what is at least ideological reassurance and is possibly the urge to take specific action. In the case of the United States in 1939, the action might be buying government bonds or volunteering for military service. Just these kind of plays, and especially films, were to come soon enough onto the American scene in the 1940s, and Henry Luce, perhaps, should be credited belatedly as American capitalism's answer to György Lukács.

If Clare Boothe Luce's essential lifetime theme can be defined as "Wake up, you lazy Americans!" her technique can be seen operating a bit differently in her most successful play, *The Women* (657 performances in 1936–7, film version 1939). Luce wrote in a preface that the real women who inspired this play "deserved to be smacked across the head with a meat-axe" and that she put them in "this little Doomsday book" to rid herself of their "hauntingly ungracious images."[39] *The Women* is unusual among plays of the depression in the sharpness of its comic attack, reminiscent in a way of the satirical grotesque pioneered by playwrights like Jonson and Wycherley and by artists like Hogarth and Bruegel. The grotesque arises in Luce's

play as it does in the work of those artists: from the tension between angry attack and comic teasing. The clash between the
mockery in the work's content and the "entertainment" messages of the overall form of the piece leads to feelings of ambivalence and tension in the audience.

In fact, the ambivalence inherent in all three of Luce's plays
of the depression was a significant factor in their resonance
with culture. Not only did the figures of her analogies capture
real tensions in American life, but her placement of these paradigms in ambiguous aesthetic frameworks matched the culture's own "mood." The love–hate attitude that Luce fostered
toward the Southern belle in *Kiss the Boys Good-bye* matched
the American ambivalence toward fascism, an ambivalence
manifested in the admiring tone of press reports of the "efficient" work of Hitler and Mussolini. Similarly, *Margin for Error* mimics the cultural ambivalence about violence and war.
Boothe places the grim theme of Nazi exterminations of Jews
and intellectuals inside the conventional format of a light mystery narrative. This conflation resonates with a cultural dialogue
between those insisting on the necessity of intervention in Europe and the still-prevailing attitude that the United States
could remain safe and productive, across her two oceans.

The Women is essentially a play about wealth and the wealthy,
and Boothe's mixing of bitter attack with elements of farce
echoed America's ambivalent feelings about those subjects.
Americans of the depression were chronically torn between
condemnation of the wealthy (Roosevelt's "money-changers in
the temple") and a desire to be rich themselves. *The Women*
captured this tension quite exactly: It offered both a biting portrait and a kind of fantasy of the cleverness and joyful excess
of the well-to-do (the luncheons, the beauty treatments, Crystal speaking on the phone from her bathtub). Crystal, as the

shop-girl who steals a rich husband, was both a model of vi-
ciousness and a figure with whom common people could empa-
thize. For a time, she beats the rich and clever people at their
own game and is only undone when she allows herself to be
lulled into complacency. Certainly, she is a callous "up-start,"
but Americans tend to identify with upstarts. Crystal is a special version of the Alger myth; audiences would tend to agree
with her when she says to the "nice" society matron, "Why
should you be the only one to sit in a tub of butter?"

It is in this ambivalence about the moral lives of the characters that *The Women* finds its resemblance to Restoration
comedy. The playwright's attitude toward the behavior of the
characters is rarely clear in any of these plays. They contain a
powerful ambivalence, a tension among admiration, wish-
fulfillment, and satire. There is a resemblance between the social world, the sexual and intellectual indiscretions dramatized
by the Restoration playwrights and the one Luce satirized in
The Women. The playwright knew this world quite thoroughly, having observed it for years from her perch as caption writer for *Vogue* and, later, managing editor at *Vanity Fair*.[40] It's
important to note that Luce's attacks in *Kiss the Boys Good-bye*
and *The Women* are not on wealthy people per se, but on their
silliness and stupidity. Luce was a self-professed hater of stupidity – in fact, John Mason Brown once described her plays
as "hating parties" – and she saw American culture as apt to
fall into two different varieties of stupidity: superficial cleverness and feigned innocence.[41] These national dangers were represented in the characters of her satire – manifested in the
pointless maneuverings and wisecracks of the "hackneyed"
characters, and in the myopic "niceness" ("too damned nice,
nice and stupid") of the central character in *The Women*.[42] The
ideological dynamic of the plays, then, is not limited simply to

a critique, ambiguous as it is, of wealthy Park Avenue women or of Hollywood moguls, but can be extended analogically to a broader theme. In each case, she is attacking (while at the same time admiring) images of America's ruling class as being, on the one hand, uselessly preoccupied with a self-destructive cleverness and, on the other hand, subject to a pretended innocence.

Luce saw herself throughout the permutations of her career as an unsentimental "realist" whose mission was to save American culture from these twin evils. She turned against Wendell Willkie (the 1940 Republican presidential nominee) during the early 1940s because of his embrace of the idea of a democratic world government in a postwar world. When he asked her opinion of the plan, she responded that he should "stop drinking, lose forty pounds and adopt a more realistic understanding of the Communists' announced plan to conquer the world."[43] Luce's first speech on the floor of Congress (9 February 1943) further illustrated her hard-line defense posture. The speech was a withering attack on Vice-President Henry Wallace's proposal that one way to ensure world peace after the war was to declare a policy of Freedom of the Skies, under which planes of all nations would have access to any airport in any country. Luce ridiculed Wallace's utopian vision, calling his attempt at "global thinking" so much "globaloney," no matter "how you slice it."[44] Mr. Wallace's seductive "warp of sense and his woof of nonsense" could be trusted to bring about the nation's defeat in the next war, when the members of Congress would hear the sound of wings:

the wings of the chickens coming home to roost, but to roost uncertainly in these steel girders above us, as the bombs of the enemy send them squawking in terror, and us squealing with shame out of this great hall.

Though these remarks occurred as part of a lengthy and largely statistical speech, it was the rhetoric of the "hard-line realist" that won her the attention of the press (even Katharine Hepburn was asked in a celebrity interview to comment on Luce's "globaloney" speech) and a cadre of adoring right-wing fans.[45] The criticisms she had made of softheaded "Marxist" intellectuals in *Kiss the Boys Good-bye* extended naturally to attacks on the Roosevelt administration, once her political career was officially launched. In a 1941 speech to the Connecticut Republican Convention, Luce warned the nation of "Communist strangulation by underground American forces spawned, nurtured, and encouraged by the Roosevelt New Deal misrepresentation."[46] This intellectual obssesion was still with Luce as late as 1977, when she attacked President Jimmy Carter ("fresh from his Georgia farm") for his attempts at détente with the Soviet Union. Mr. Carter, she wrote in *The National Review*,

has no more idea of what détente is really about than do the majority of his countrymen. Détente is about the voluntary U.S. retreat from geopolitical power and the U.S. acceptance of the geopolitical advance of the Soviet Union.[47]

Luce continued her vigilance against cocktail-party subversives and Soviet aggression even into her eighties, serving on President Reagan's advisory panel on covert operations.[48]

As a rare example of a successful comic writer who gave up writing to go into politics, Luce's life and work shows a surprising seamlessness. The doubleness was organic, the policy maven living inside the society wit all along, like a dybbuk, occasionally stressing the Bergdorf Goodman fabric, but for the most part just speaking pointedly through the perfect mouth. The cohabitation was in fact grotesque, of course, and eventually the dybbuk took over entirely, smothering the comedienne

1 — 35237

Donna Page

OCLC
34590918

amazon.com

| WELCOME | BOOKS | | | | | YOUR ACCOUNT | HELP | | SELL ITEMS |

| BOOK SEARCH | BROWSE SUBJECTS | BESTSELLERS | FEATURED IN THE MEDIA | AWARD WINNERS | MUSIC | VIDEO | TOYS & GAMES | ELECTRONICS | e-CARDS | COMPUTERS & INTERNET | KIDS | AUCTIONS | BUSINESS & INVESTING | zSHOPS |

Book Information

Rediscovering China : Dynamics and Dilemmas of Reform

by Cheng Li, A. Doak Barnett

Our Price: $19.95

at a glance

reviews

customer comments

if you like this book...

table of contents

Availability: Usually ships within 24 hours.
Paperback - (September 1997) 376 pages

Customer Comments
Write an online review and share your thoughts with other readers!

Add to Shopping Cart
(you can always remove it later)

Shopping with us is 100% safe. Guaranteed.

one day in 1940 and parading thereafter in her clothes. When called upon to create an "updated" version of *The Women* in 1966, the dybbuk was revealed: Every new joke fell flat and the "revised ending" of the play (a bout of hair-pulling between two defeated villainesses) was an appalling disaster.[49]

S. N. Behrman

The remarkable success during the depression of S. N. Behrman's thoroughly serious comedies adds to the picture of a cultural moment especially hungry for an ambivalent, difficult kind of aesthetic experience. Behrman's comedies do not provide the conventional rewards that one expects from comedies successful in the commercial American theatre. They are relentlessly hard and intellectual; they consistently avoid the sentimental closure that would leave a popular audience feeling that all was right with the world. Walter Kerr once labeled the conventional, sentimental tying up in Neil Simon's plays as the "big hug theory of dramaturgy"; it is the hug that dissolves the comic problem into the complacent goo of melodrama. Behrman did not offer any "big hugs" to his audience in the 1930s. His plays brought together and set against one another, in the form of character "types," the dominant intellectual and moral forces of the decade. His serious comedies were dramatic paradigms for the cultural dilemmas of the 1930s.

Behrman's metaphor for Western culture in crisis took the unlikely form of the comfortable drawing room of a wealthy household. Krutch called these theatrical spaces, which by 1932 had become inevitable in a Behrman play, "realistic substitutes for a spot of enchanted ground upon which deadly enemies can meet."[50] Into these Racinean spaces walk characters who make no bones about "standing for" the essential forces in conflict in the period; threatened capitalists, hard-line communists, well-meaning liberals, fascists, parasitic socialites, and frustrated artists arrange and rearrange themselves in a slow dance through Behrman's six original comedies of the depression. They air their points of view and engage in intellectual combat within Behrman's thin plots in a kind of distillation of the crisis of Western culture.

Unlike the plays of Sherwood or Luce, Behrman's plays are not particularly "funny" in the sense of containing discrete jokes. Behrman was capable of writing wisecracks – a quality that comes through in the character of Dennis, a smart-aleck representative of liberal Catholicism in *End of Summer* – but he typically steered away from this kind of dialogue, preferring to sustain long and balanced passages of give-and-take between opposing forces. Behrman employed variations on the same basic narrative in nearly every one of his plays: A "fascinating" woman of liberal tendencies is sought after by both a communist and a fascist; she rebuffs both ideologies (and the persons of both suitors) and resolves to remain an optimistic freethinker.[51]

The reason for the success of Behrman's plays, plays so lacking in conventional rewards of sentiment or laughter, lay in the accuracy of his construction of this analogy for the cultural dilemma of the 1930s, an analogy carried out in both the general form of the plays and in the content of the narratives. In his juxtaposition of threatening issues and folly, Behrman pressed the comic contract to its limits. In *Rain from Heaven* (100 performances, 1934) a Jewish refugee's moral dilemma of whether or not to return to Germany and sacrifice himself in a fight against Hitler is juxtaposed with his involvement in a silly love triangle that would be at home in any romantic comedy.

Though *Rain from Heaven* is the most extreme example of a grotesque demand on his audiences, as they are pulled now to fear and pity and then to comic distance, it is characteristic of the aesthetic peculiarity of Behrman's plays: He offers characters with choices that may result in dire consequences. Moreover, in many cases, they go off to suffer those consequences. Willens, the refugee, returns to almost certain death in Germany. In *End of Summer* (152 performances, 1936), the lovable grandmother dies, the young people all are demoralized by unemployment, and Leonie (the "irresistible woman") is deprived of all illusions about herself in a painful, cruel scene that summons images, in the contemporary reader, of the shattering of Blanche Dubois. Leonie descends the stairs of her country house, wearing her mother's wedding gown, swirling and primping, lost in a romantic haze about the beauty that has been lost in the world (Figure 9). Leonie's daughter interrupts the reverie, and tricks the megalomaniac psychiatrist who had been exploiting Leonie for her money into admitting that he does not love Leonie; rather, he wants to marry Paula, the daughter. Leonie flees to her room to "lie down," only to return within moments because she cannot bear the thoughts that come crashing down on her. She mourns her lack of realism, saying, "I suppose the thing about me that is wrong is that love is really all I care about."[52] Meanwhile, the Machiavellian psychiatrist (Kenneth) has been dispatched, and the final scene between him and the daughter (Paula) is paradigmatic Behrman. Paula completes the journey that Behrman wishes upon his liberal characters in the 1930s: from high-minded idealism to hard-nosed dealing. She leaves the fantasy world of abstract goodness and accepts the world as it is – the battleground, at least at present, between skillful evildoers and those who, like herself, oppose them. In so real and climactic a battle, the fighters for good cannot afford to be softheaded. In their last encounter, after Kenneth's defeat, the two become more than simply individual characters; they speak as archetypes for the great conflict of the world. "I suppose you're going to tell me this isn't cricket," Paula says to Kenneth. "Well, don't, because it will only make me laugh. To live up to a code with people like you is only to be weak and absurd" (p. 236). The psychiatrist, his voice "low and even but tense with hate," assures Paula that she is his "*last* miscalculation." The scene can be viewed as Behrman's declaration that social graces and good manners, the civilizing forces that he had previously recommended in his plays, would be of no use in defeating fascism. In fact, notions of "fair play" would need to be temporarily abandoned.

His change in attitude seems tied to his intense concern in 1936 for the safety of Jews in Europe. Behrman was involved at the time with Elza Heifetz, daughter of the violin virtuoso, and the two were married later in that year. The Heifetzes, intimately in touch with European colleagues and relatives, were a well-informed and passionate source of private reporting about the nightmare unfolding in Europe. In *The Burning Glass*, the autobiographical novel that Behrman published in 1968, the author has his fictional stand-in, David Grant, writing *End of Summer* while attending the Salzburg Festival.[53] Behrman and Heifetz did in reality attend the festival, but Behrman has reworked the chronology of events; their disturbing Austrian trip actually took place in 1937, the year after the play was written.[54] In the novel, Grant conceives the play while on a train crossing Germany, basing it upon events he had witnessed the pre-

Figure 9. The crisis distilled to the drawing room: Osgood Perkins, Ina Claire, and Doris Dudley in S. N. Behrman's *End of Summer* (1936). (New York Public Library)

vious year while in close contact with a wealthy family who had a house on the coast of Maine. A vulnerable and love-seeking woman had been exploited by a manipulative doctor, who had maneuvered the woman into leaving her entire fortune to his research institute. The woman had then died unexpectedly, and the doctor was rumored to have somehow brought about her demise. Still, Grant intends to make this story into a comedy, a task that he was sure he could accomplish because "he had no intention of letting Mrs. Frobisher die" (p. 27). She would be rescued from the doctor by her daughter. The fictional play-wright planned to set his play

in the midst of the depression, when even the rich Frobishers felt in-secure, and to populate their house on the masculine Riviera with her daughter's friends – young, bright, rebellious and unemployed. It was the passing of an era in America too. (p. 41)

Arriving in Salzburg, the events of the Maine story mingle in his mind with what he sees and feels in the Nazi-controlled city. He stays in the enormous home of the actress that he plans to cast in the central role of the play, and he becomes obsessed by an analogy between the woman in Maine and this actress – who is being driven from her home because she is of Jewish an-cestry. Both women had been "deprived of their heritage by a sinister and uncontrollable force" (p. 27). Unable to sleep that first night in Salzburg, he awakens to see a group of hooded men using lime to burn a gigantic swastika into his hostess's lawn. Grant joins the servants at dawn, scrubbing at the hid-eous sign with a brush, hoping that the sensitive woman would never see it. The damage to the lawn would be explained as "a blight" (p. 40). When Grant goes into town for a haircut, he feels that everyone senses that he is a Jew. He fears for a mo-ment that the barber might cut his throat.

As he continues to work on the play in Salzburg, surrounded by hatred and a sense of doom, the personal story of the Maine family merges with the actress's life in Austria. Grant's play bcomes infused with a political meaning, so much so that the author worries that the play will veer too far away from comedy:

He began to suspect the validity of the whole conception on which he was basing his play. It was all true, it had all happened, but could he make it seem true in the theater? Wouldn't it emerge as melodrama? On the Arlberg Express he was sure he had it, but now the edifice crumbled. (pp. 41–2)

In life, the playwright does manage to end the play, like all of Behrman's comedies, with a kind of merry resignation. Having rejected the doctor's attempts to recoup his losses, Leonie sets about investing her money in "Young America," the radical magazine that her daughter's friends are starting. She and the funniest of the radical young people end the play in banter about the magazine, and a drink:

LEONIE: I suppose if it's really successful – it'll result in my losing everything I have –

DENNIS: It'll be taken from you anyway. You'll only be anticipating the inevitable.

LEONIE: Why – how clever of me!

DENNIS: Not only clever but graceful.

LEONIE: Will you leave me just a little to live on – ?

DENNIS: Don't worry about that – come the Revolution – you'll have a friend in high office.

> [*LEONIE accepts gratefully this earnest of security. They touch glasses in a toast as the curtain falls.*]   (pp. 255–6)

The creative process that Behrman fictionalized in *The Burning Glass* enlivens an understanding of Behrman's nearly impossible mixtures. The narrative shows that he himself was painfully aware of dark material that he was pouring into the comic form. Like the playwright he presents in *No Time for Comedy*, he has struggled with the awful state of the world and has accepted that he can only do with it what his talent allows: create comedies that will somehow, if unsteadily, turn horror into a smile, doom into determination (Figure 10). This conflation of dire events with comic convention matched the cultural situation of Americans in the 1930s, and audiences consistently warmed to these plays – works that seem, to a later generation, strangely irrelevant, anachronistic, unkempt. Facing bad news, fearful events, humiliations at every turn, Americans of the thirties bounced along on Willy Loman's "smile and a shoeshine," following the (probably psychologically necessary) cultural messages to "buy another cup of coffee, and smile, smile, smile." Audiences may also have made an unconscious connection between the situation of Behrman's omnipresent "fascinating woman" and the struggle within their own minds. The woman in those representative drawing rooms, alternately attracted by the muscularity and order of the fascist and by the steely righteousness of the communist, stands for the mentality of the American middle class. Eventually seeing both suitors in a realistic light, and calling on a seemingly innate store of courage and skepticism, she experiences a moment of illumination that allows her to pull free from the appeals of both suitors and persevere in a freewheeling way of life, intelligent and energetic, unguided by any program save her own instinct and reason.

This "wooing" analogy was flattering to its audience, and encouraging. Through it, Behrman communicated an attractive

Figure 10. The anxious comedian: Laurence Olivier in Behr-man's *No Time for Comedy* (1939). (New York Public Library)

image of the American psyche, and his myth shows America triumphing by remaining "as it truly is" – a "true" identity that Behrman associates exclusively with liberal democracy. It is a reassuring myth, outlining an alternative path to revolution of one kind or another, assuring America that its intellectual foundations and native tendencies are good, to be trusted, and adequate to the present challenge.

A convincing proof of the psychic linkage of Behrman's plays to the specific dilemma of their cultural moment lies in the completeness of their disappearance from the repertoire with the advent of World War II. In spite of his almost universal acclaim in the thirties as one of the foremost American playwrights – Krutch wrote that he had "as sure a position in the contemporary American theatre as any writer can claim"[55] – Behrman is produced and read even less than the other faded "star" of the thirties – Maxwell Anderson. Behrman's plays do not, however, present the artistic problems of a playwright like Anderson, who – struggling to fulfill a Romantic ideal of "importance" – concocted plays that were perfect targets for deflation. The plays of S. N. Behrman may strike the contemporary reader as somewhat redundant and overlong, but their dialogue is still crisp and their ideas as clearly argued as when the plays were first performed. The reason for their disappearance is more subtle: The cultural dilemma that they reified in their mixed form and narrative symbolism was jerked out of contention in December 1941, and with that cultural shift Behrman's analogies were rendered largely irrelevant.[56]

William Saroyan

William Saroyan's *The Time of Your Life* (185 performances, 1939) has fared considerably better, perhaps because the analogy he offered with his existential saloon was more universal. The play is undeniably linked to the cultural situation of the thirties – with Detective Blick as cryptofascist, Kit Carson an embodiment of American "frontier spirit," and so on – but the characters are removed far enough from realism that they take on an enduring significance. *The Time of Your Life* is grotesque in the tension it maintains among sentiment, humor, and threat. Saroyan managed here to suspend in a whimsical solution symbolic representatives of the threats to the culture (fascism, crime, unemployment, technology) along with balancing markers for what he saw as America's saving graces (tradition, compassion, humor).

There is a sense in the play, to quote a Christian truism, that "all things work together unto good." This mystical variety of optimism reflected Saroyan's own feelings about the depression. He liked to call this period the "Great Uppression" because he felt it was a time when things kept getting better and better, "a beautiful time, and the fraudulence of the world couldn't diminish the beauty."[57] This attitude toward the history of the period – reflective of an irritating and characteristic solipsism on Saroyan's part, as it was based on his feelings about his own career, which flourished during the thirties – no doubt contributed to the popular success of the play. It resonated with the willful optimism so exemplified by Dale Carnegie's *How to Win Friends and Influence People*, one of the bestselling books of the decade. Saroyan's barroom Irishman, Joe, would make a star Carnegie pupil. He is assertive; he is sincerely interested in others; he gives others *sincere compliments* – Carnegie's magic formula. Saroyan struggled to repeat this formula in his other plays, but he never again hit upon the balance of threat and assurance that led to the cultural resonance of *The Time of Your Life*. A notoriously undisciplined writer, one who relied on vague inspirations more than on craft, he tended in his other work to leave threat out entirely or to give its representatives no power; instead, the plays concern whimsical and uniformly "good" people, afloat in vague worlds governed by a fatuous sentimentality.

Arsenic and Old Lace

John Lahr has written convincingly on Noel Coward's *Blithe Spirit* as a therapeutic instrument in the social psychology of wartime England. That play also enjoyed a popular acceptance in the American commercial theatre (257 performances on Broadway in 1941–2), and much of Lahr's argument that the play provides its audience with mechanisms for dealing with the sudden deaths of loved ones can also be applied to the play's appeal in North America.[58] Lahr's rejection of the traditional understanding of farce as entertainment that leads people to "forget their troubles" through a zany distraction is just as applicable to *Arsenic and Old Lace,* a play that also opened at the outset of America's involvement in the war in 1941.

Arsenic and Old Lace is distinct from the body of farce that dominated the stage in the thirties. The play's grotesque pairings and desperate consequences set it apart from the sentimentality of Kaufman's creations like *You Can't Take It with You* or the detached triviality of George Abbott products like *Three Men on a Horse* or *Brother Rat.* Joseph Kesselring's macabre mixture of murder, torture, and romance is by now quite familiar to American audiences, for the play has become a staple in the repertoire of amateur companies across the country. For audiences of the depression, however, the play carried a power to shock and surprise. Upon its opening, a critic for *PM* wrote that "the theatre, which is several thousand years old, has never produced anything like *Arsenic and Old Lace*."[59]

It is possible that with our familiarity with the narrative we have become partially inured to the play's psychological effects. Moreover, the steady twentieth-century diet of filmed "black comedies" about murder and the handling of dead bodies (*The Trouble with Harry, The Wrong Box, Vacation, Eating Raoul, Scenes from the Class Struggle in Beverly Hills, Beetlejuice*, and so on) could be expected to have furthered our resistance to the comparatively tame effects of *Arsenic and Old Lace*. Still, the play carries a peculiar power, and its enormous popularity cannot be given over entirely to the appeal of its witty dialogue. In the environment of the late depression and the outbreak of what threatened to be a devastating world war, Kesselring hit upon a narrative that proved profoundly attractive to American culture.

Arsenic and Old Lace was developed between 1937, when Kesselring sold the script to Howard Lindsay and Russel Crouse, and January of 1941, when it opened in New York. At the play's opening, critics were nearly unanimous in praising it, Richard Lockridge commenting that "You wouldn't believe homicidal mania could be such fun!"[60] The play proved an immediate success, running for three years before moving into the lucrative amateur market. The narrative found its largest single audience when Frank Capra's popular film version, closely adapted from the play, was released in 1944.

The writing and initial popularity of *Arsenic and Old Lace* coincided with the peak of America's anxiety about involvement in a world war. The long years of public anguish over the worsening situations in Europe and the Pacific turned to a sharp internal debate in 1939 and 1940 about whether and how the United States could avoid entering into the conflict. Isolationism had prevailed throughout the depression and was the essential issue of the 1940 election; the Republicans charged in radio spots that Roosevelt was eager to send American youths to their deaths. The ads, sponsored by the Republican National Committee, although never endorsed by Willkie, warned:

When your boy is dying on some battlefield in Europe . . . and he's crying out, 'Mother! Mother!' – don't blame Franklin D. Roosevelt because he sent your boy to war – blame YOURSELF because you sent Franklin D. Roosevelt back to the White House![61]

In response to this kind of rhetoric, Roosevelt was goaded into promising at every campaign stop that "your boys are not going to be sent into any foreign war." Even as late as May of 1940 – with Hitler's army arrayed across much of Europe and with news of the mass persecution of Jews, church workers, and others creeping into the pages of the daily papers – only 36 percent of Americans favored helping England if it meant risking U.S. involvement. The public attitude was volatile, however; by December of 1940, with England severely threatened by the Axis onslaught, the percentage in favor of sending weaponry was 60 percent.[62] A few weeks before the play opened, Roosevelt initiated the lend–lease program, and the country teetered on the brink of war throughout the play's first year in production, with the population in a frantic and expectant state that was not resolved until the bombing of Pearl Harbor in December 1941. Now it was no longer a foreign war.

Arsenic and Old Lace offered devices for the relief of America's fears. The play conjured theatrical symbols for the threatening figures and abstract fears of the national mind and displayed them finally dispatched at the hands of the audience's own representative – Mortimer, a professional drama critic. Through the experience of this play, audiences could externalize their tremendous anxieties about war, murder, and death within the safe context of light entertainment. The play led them to laugh at fear itself.

The essential trick of *Arsenic and Old Lace,* of course, is to make murder funny, something Kesselring manages through the familiar comic techniques of inversion and exaggeration. The two nice old aunts are not just murderers, but mass murderers; Jonathan is not simply a deviant and murderer, but a kind of monster from a horror film. Beyond this, the play's metaphorical work is complex and, in part, ambiguous. The clearest part has to do with Mortimer's brother, Jonathan.

In a pattern like the one guiding so many fairy tales, *Arsenic and Old Lace* features paired opposites, with Jonathan functioning as Mortimer's evil twin. The monster Jonathan stands as a nightmare vision of what Mortimer could become should he succumb to the family's hereditary madness; and since Mortimer is the audience member's representative, his fate has a wider significance. Like Hitler, Jonathan is maniacal, raving; he kills for the pleasure of it. He is accompanied by a mad scientist – Dr. Einstein! – whose attempts to alter Jonathan's appearance have turned him into a monster, said to resemble Boris Karloff. Mortimer tries to frighten Jonathan away, but Jonathan seems about to prevail. He has Mortimer bound and prepared to be tortured to death (Figure 11); but Mortimer is freed by the bumbling efforts of the police, Dr. Einstein escapes, and Jonathan is arrested (Figure 12).

Mortimer's triumph over Jonathan offered a vital and comforting narrative to audiences of 1940–4. Throughout the 1930s, Germany developed a role in America's national mentality as the "dark side" version of the United States: the "other" great

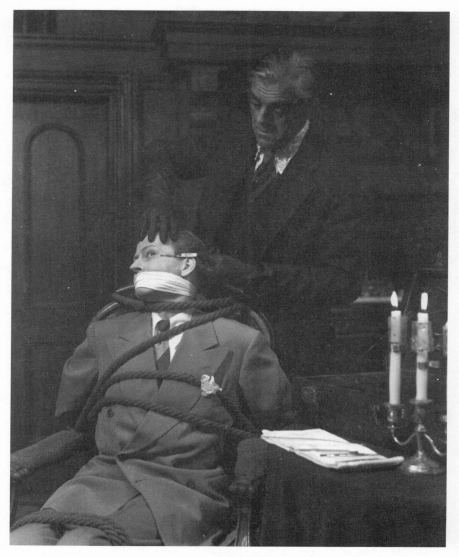

Figure 11. The original monster at play: Boris Karloff (Jonathan) prepares to operate on Allyn Joslyn (Mortimer) in Kesselring's *Arsenic and Old Lace* (1941). (New York Public Library)

Figure 12. The alternative monster captured: Bela Lugosi as
Jonathan Brewster, with Jack Whiting as Mortimer (on stairs)
in Kesselring's *Arsenic and Old Lace* (1942). (New York Public
Library)

power of the West, led by a raving man, apparently mad and known to be killing wantonly. Mortimer's fear that he will "turn into" Jonathan expresses the nation's fear of "turning into" Germany, in the sense of being swept – with the demands of war – into the kind of mass hysteria that Americans had watched as it overtook Germany in the thirties. That phenomenon had alarmed Americans throughout the decade with the apparent irrationality of it all: How could a country of intelligent people be so attracted by what seemed to most Americans an utterly repellant figure? What could not be understood – a seeming national madness – was a dangerous force loose in the world. It could strike anywhere.

The literature of the thirties displays an obsession with the possibility of a fascist triumph in the United States. Sinclair Lewis's presentation of exactly this transformation, *It Can't Happen Here*, was among the best-selling novels of the decade, and the nationwide performances of the dramatic version by the Federal Theatre Project added up to the equivalent of a five-year run. In addition to Boothe's *Kiss the Boys Good-bye* and *Margin for Error*, other plays warned of the potential for a Nazi-like party to take over the country: The hero of Kaufman and Hart's patriotic melodrama, *The American Way* (1939), is killed for interrupting a local Nazi rally; left-wing plays like Lawson's *Marching Song* (1937) or Lillian Hellman's *Days to Come* (1936) portray Nazi-like groups arising as enforcers for business interests.

This great national anxiety on the part of Americans, a nation's fear of madness, is worked out in the narrative of Kesselring's grotesque farce: Mortimer discovers that he is no blood relation to Jonathan after all. The moment of this revelation is one of joyous relief both for Mortimer and the audience. When his aunts tell him that he is, in truth, the son of an unwed woman who was once their cook, Mortimer announces joyfully, "I'm a bastard!" and his fiancée "leaps into his arms."[63] Jonathan is captured and sent off to incarceration, and Mortimer is free from his fear of transformation. He will remain brash and happy-go-lucky and can marry the minister's plucky daughter.

The narrative function of the aunts is more difficult to define. We both identify with them and agree with Mortimer that they need to be stopped in as humane a way as possible. They are lovable, of course, and murderers. The motivation for their murders has a kind of attraction; they are killing people, but out of the best intentions. They face the notion and physical reality of death with an enviable casualness (think of Martha's discovery of the body in the window seat), but they are frightened and powerless in the face of the threat posed by Jonathan.

Considering all of this, the aunts can be seen to stand, apart from Mortimer, for another part of the American psyche. Related to the fear of "turning into" Germany was the fear of evil growing from what seemed to be good, the nagging doubt about isolationism. Could it be that a persistence in neutrality, a policy that seemed on the surface to be so moral and humane, would lead to a greater conflagration than would intervention? Was "peace at any price" a slogan for the destruction for the human race? The popular press of the thirties was full of disdain for Neville Chamberlain and his policy of "appeasement." The policy was seen as a sugar-coated poison that had contributed to Hitler's boldness against his neighbors and his abuse of Germany's own population. In this light, the isolationist position, while seemingly a peaceful one, was in fact an unintentional prescription for the deaths of millions.

The aunts can be seen as the nation's nightmare version of the isolationists: Acting out of a seemingly "good" emotional motivation, they go about killing people "for their own good."

They are the sentimental current in the American character
that could lead the country into drastic, irresponsible error. "It
may not be charitable of me," says Aunt Abby, "but I've almost
come to the conclusion that this Mr. Hitler isn't a Christian."
They act without reference to discipline or conceptual knowl-
edge of a social good. They are the raw, emotional, self-assured
element in the national mentality that we feel about ourselves
and that has its attractive aspects, but that we do not trust.
From their own perspective, their actions seem perfectly logical and moral.

The aunts need to be controlled by the logic and social reference of our representative, Mortimer, who knows that sentimentality must be overcome if evil is to be defeated. Garry
Wills has described this very process that was taking place in
the America of 1940–1: the nation convincing itself of the need
for "total war."[64] At the very time that *Arsenic and Old Lace*
opened, the United States was undergoing a psychological sea
change, from sentimental and old-fashioned isolationism to the
hardness necessary to defeat evil. The country achieved, as
Wills put it,

that most refined of pleasures, a virtuous hate. Killing for an idea is
the worst kind of killing. Better to hate a person, the assailant of one's
family or home, than to hate an idea. What if the idea hides behind
an otherwise law-abiding and unmenacing exterior? Then one must
steel oneself against all normal amenities and personal attraction.
Then one launches a crusade – to be followed by an inquisition. (pp.
14–15)

The aunts do win a temporary victory in the conclusion of
the narrative as they prepare to poison Mr. Witherspoon – who
has come to take them to a humane confinement. It is a kind
of "play" victory, however, giving the audience pleasure in see-

ing the sentimental but dangerous figures winning a "pretend" triumph in a context of safety. This release is safe because we know full well that, even if they do poison Mr. Witherspoon, Mortimer (the figure of rationality) will ultimately prevail and the sisters will be locked up in Happy Dale. The real dangers have been defeated: The figure of reason is secure in his separation from the irrational parts; the raging, "evil" aspect of the national personality has been subdued; and the sweetly deceptive version of that same force has been spotted and is soon to be placed under constraint. We can laugh at this last adventure of the deadly sentimental figures because we know that reason is ultimately in control.

Thus the play worked a kind of dream therapy on its audience. They could leave the theatre with a sense that confusion about the national identity had been worked out and that right order would prevail. As in the case of the other mixed comedies of the depression, this metaphorical theatrical experience matched the political tensions of the era, and its playing eased a gnawing sense of conflict within the national self. It was an experience for which people hungered.

3

Misery Burlesqued
The Peculiar Case of
Tobacco Road

CONSIDERING THE UNIVOCAL EARNESTNESS that
one expects in "realistic" (that is, illusionistic) attempts
at persuasion, the American "social drama" of the
1930s would not seem a fertile ground for the grotesque. The
grotesque, with its inherent tendencies toward self-contradiction
and deflation, is antithetical to the sustained expression of an
earnest "realism." It is not surprising, then, that it was these
very elements in the social dramas of the thirties that were indicated as flaws by left-wing critics who accepted the doctrine of
socialist realism formulated by Lunacharsky and rendered as

dogma by Joseph Stalin.[1] "Social" plays were not to be ambiguous or mixed or formally disruptive; such devices only "confused" the masses, who required understandable (and so "realistic") depictions of the evils of the present system and of a clear path to change.

If popularity is any guide, however, the grotesque found its strongest resonance with depression culture in a quirky play that managed to work as a social drama while breaking all the canonical rules, combining its naturalistic interests with incidents more closely related to slapstick comedy and sex farce. The stage version of Erskine Caldwell's *Tobacco Road* was an odd and persistently controversial play that was seen by over three million paying customers across the country at a time when most Americans had little expendable income. Its enormous success was puzzling to many intellectuals of the period and became the subject of a prolonged debate.

From the beginning, the creators of *Tobacco Road* touted the play for its social usefulness, insisting on its "documentary" qualities. It is true that *Tobacco Road* has some things in common with a "social" aesthetic. The play does portray people in a wretched state – a world stereotypically identified with socially conscious naturalism in the tradition of Zola, and it even includes a handful of didactic speeches about the history and plight of Southern tenant farmers. Its notorious depiction of the sexual activities of the Lesters fits into a naturalist tradition of biological determinism. Legitimate comparisons could be made between *Tobacco Road* and *Spring's Awakening, Miss Julie, The Power of Darkness, Rose Bernd, Thérèse Raquin,* and other classics in this genre. Still, something is wrong here.

Tobacco Road is hardly a simple and earnest depiction of the lives of these supposed crackers. Unlike other plays in the tradition, the stage production of *Tobacco Road* led the audience to an attitude of leering mockery toward the characters. The producers' marketing of the play presented it – on the level of overt description – as a kind of activist naturalism and – on the level of suggestion and innuendo – as a festival of sexual explicitness in a context of low humor. The marketing was symptomatic of a doubleness in the play that found a corresponding doubleness in the public response; the play had a sufficient relation to social drama that its producers could claim a high moral ground in newspaper articles about the tragic condition of the poor whites in the South at the same time that their publicity department published countless pictures of actresses in ripped costumes being grabbed from behind by leering actors.[2]

So *Tobacco Road* was a complex thing that spoke to a complex audience through a grotesque conflation of signs. It was a social drama, of a kind, and at the same time a peculiar kind of sex comedy. Through a fortuitous blend of artistic accident and sensitivity to the cultural marketplace, the creators of *Tobacco Road* assembled a product that catered to the traditional public hunger for sexual excitement and, at the same time, performed the cultural work of reducing the tremendous "poverty anxieties" of depression America. By combining elements of social drama with a voyeuristic interest in sex, and through the comic techniques of exaggeration and incongruity, *Tobacco Road* became both a "serious" drama and a hilarious burlesque of the social horrors it depicted. It proved a potent combination that satisfied a seemingly endless national demand.

The Production

Tobacco Road opened at the Masque Theatre in New York on 4 December 1933 and played continuously in New York until

May of 1941.[3] The play, based on the novel that Erskine Caldwell had published the previous year, was adapted for the stage
by Jack Kirkland, whose previous work included the unsuccessful melodrama *Frankie and Johnny* (1930) and the scenario
for a Hollywood musical, *Heads Up* (1930). Early in the run,
Kirkland – who was coproducer of the show – engaged Michael
Goldreyer as publicity director; thereafter Goldreyer's name
appeared frequently in the dramatic columns and, as the touring companies began to meet injunctions and demonstrations,
in news stories as well.[4]

Kirkland remained the guiding figure behind the production
machinery throughout its run and was the initiator of the touring companies that traveled the country from 1935 to 1942; the
tours brought in a gross earning of $3 million and, together
with the $2.5 million gross of the New York production, made
Tobacco Road one of the most profitable plays that had ever
been produced.[5] The original investment was said to have been
just six thousand dollars.[6]

Considering that the New York ticket price for the play never exceeded two dollars, with balcony seats for as little as one
dollar, and that the prices on tour ranged from a dollar and a
half to fifty cents – and taking into account the repeat atten-
dance to which Goldreyer referred almost obsessively – the production was seen by between three and a half million and four
million people.[7] The record-breaking run of the Broadway production stood at 3,182 performances, not to be exceeded until
Life with Father passed that mark in June of 1947.[8] However,
by the time of its closing on Broadway, *Tobacco Road* had become more than a profitable piece of theatre; it had become a
kind of cultural icon. Its title was by then part of the national
vocabulary: the phrase "Tobacco Road" was generally used to
apply comic derision to a place or a group of people.

The peculiar double nature of the play encouraged the myths that Michael Goldreyer set about constructing in the public imagination and that Kirkland and Caldwell augmented in frequent newspaper articles. They said that the costumes were actual "barrel clothes" that had been sent south as charity; they said that the audience at the performance in Augusta were near-duplicates of the characters on stage. Stories circulated about the effects of the production on the cast: that their feet had spread out from not wearing shoes, that they were raising vegetables in the dirt on stage, that they kidded one another by putting goldfish in the drinking water, that their teeth were wearing down from eating raw turnips. Glamorous and seminude photographs were released to the press to "prove" that the actresses who portrayed Ellie Mae were ravishing beauties before applying the disfiguring makeup.[9] The claims for the production became so extreme and wide-ranging that *Tobacco Road* came to take on a titanic quality in the public mind, a sort of lowbrow *Gesamtkunstwerk*. It is difficult even to imagine a mere piece of theatre that could be worthy of an advertisement that claimed it to be

The modern American stage classic . . . the most discussed stage play in the history of the theatre . . . one of the outstanding contributions to the dramatic literature of the century . . . required as extra-curricular reading in the English Departments of sixteen colleges and universities . . . endorsed by ministers . . . the only play ever to cause a resolution to be introduced into Congress . . . *Tobacco Road* is the portrayal of the lives of people, neglected by the government and by civilization for centuries, living in squalor and poverty, ignorant of everything except sex and religion and dreaming of the days when prosperity will return to their farm land. . . . Although primarily a serious study of these people in their own environment, a careful check has disclosed 200 hearty laughs in the performance.[10]

The question arose frequently as to whether *Tobacco Road* was intended by its authors to be funny at all, and the controversy that ensued on this question testifies to the doubleness of the play and of the public response (Figure 13). There were those who chose to see the play exclusively as a social drama. For them, the source of the production's "200 hearty laughs" was typically seen as a corruption by the actors of an essentially "serious" text. An article that appeared in the *New York Times* during the final weeks of the Broadway run featured an interview with Francis L. DeVallant, a businessman who had seen the play thirty-four times. DeVallant preferred the early performances featuring Henry Hull as Jeeter Lester because "the play started getting more comic, less tragic, when James Barton went into it."[11] In a similar vein, Lloyd Lewis wrote of one of the touring companies in 1941:

Under the wear and tear of so much usage, *Tobacco Road* has changed a lot since Broadway first saw it. Most of the inner shadings, much of its social meaning, and many of Henry Hull's subtler phases of characterization have disappeared. Today the play is mainly a burlesque of cracker depravity. The broader humor of the text still survives, but the earthiness of the text is now merely sooty.[12]

To look at the authors' own statements about the play is to watch a delicate dance. From early in the play's run, Kirkland and Caldwell persistently claimed that they intended the play to be funny and, at the same time, horrible. They claimed that the play revealed ugly conditions, and they listed various justifications for its undeniable comedy. Jack Kirkland, in an article that appeared in 1939, placed "Humor" as the first in his list of reasons for the play's long run and "Timeliness" as the fourth. His discussion of the play's humor is oblique, but he

Figure 13. Fear resolved by mockery: Henry Hull and Ruth
Hunter in *Tobacco Road* (1933). (New York Public Library)

seems to imply that it is intended to make the play more accessible and to give it a satiric force:

1. Humor – The play is funny. Grimly funny, if you like, but very
funny, and deliberately contrived so. The trail back is a simple one
to follow. I worked a number of years in motion pictures. I have never missed laughing at a Charlie Chaplin tragedy, nor ever forgotten
one. Nietzsche said: "I have met my devil and he is the spirit of
gravity. Laughter, not anger, slayeth." You can be sure Mr. Chaplin
makes no such mistake.[13]

Caldwell consistently identified himself with the play, saying
more than once that Kirkland wrote it just as he would have
done himself, had he been a playwright. His defense of the use
of comedy in the play is similar to Kirkland's, if less grandiose.
In a preface to the play's first published version (1934), Caldwell recounted the somewhat exaggerated tale of the critics' attacking the play for being, on the one hand, vulgar, and on the
other, socially useless.[14] Then, in a most interesting paragraph,
he defends what I have called the grotesque aspects of the play
as intentional devices meant to "entrap" its audience:

This is not a perfect drama. It possesses those groping, gaping perforations which I believe to be necessary as a means of communication between author and audience. The play of glazed surface is ideal for an evening's entertainment. Playgoing then is an escape. But
in *Tobacco Road* there is no escape. Those perforations are traps set
to snare you. If you should enter into the play through one of them,
you cannot escape.[15]

The authors' statements are, of course, conditioned by their
desire to attract an audience, and it is tempting to speculate
that the humor of the play – or at least part of it – was more
the result of inept playwriting than of a Chaplinesque artistic

plan. Still, it would be unwise to dismiss their remarks as specious. One senses in them the sincere desire of artists struggling to explain for themselves a puzzling work that "got away" from them and somehow tapped into a powerful public need. They are part of a long tradition in the grotesque of artists, not entirely in control of their materials, who struggle to explain why the resulting objects "work" so well before an eager public. Like the medieval guilds, the Jacobean dramatists, Hieronymus Bosch, or even Dumas fils, Kirkland and Caldwell pull together moral and aesthetic defenses for mixing comedy and sex into a product intended to reflect and reform.

Caldwell's remarks do amount to a fair description of a work that is grotesque, disturbing, and not easily dismissed or digested, an aesthetic that Caldwell was known to admire and that he employed skillfully in his fiction. Kenneth Burke praised this quality of Caldwell's work, seeing it as part of a system of "balked religiosity" and a "cult of incongruity."[16] Caldwell's statement is all the more impressive in that he acknowledges the role of accident in opening these nondiscursive means of "communication." The work is not "perfect," he says; it is not the inevitable result of a conscious artistic plan.[17]

Secular Conversions

In an essay published in 1935, Kenneth Burke argued that psychoanalysis was helpful to people because it opened to the patient a "perspective of incongruity."[18] He saw modern psychology as part of a system of "secular conversions" whereby what had in an earlier age been called devils, and were now called anxieties, were cast out by the psychologist through his or her use of a "vocabulary of conversion," an "exorcism by misnomer" (p. 133). He offers as an example of this beneficent process the situation of an adult responding to a child's fear of a monster in the corner of his darkened room:

One goes impiously into the corner, while the child looks on aghast. One picks an old coat off the clothes rack, and one says, "Look, it's only an old coat." The child breaks into fitful giggles. Has one *named* the object which struck terror in the child? On the contrary, one has totally misnamed it, as regards its nature in the child's previous orientation. To have *named* it would have been to call out, "Away, thou hideous monster, thou cackling demon from hell, away!" and henceforth that corner would be the very altar of terror. One casts out demons by a vocabulary of *conversion,* by an *incongruous naming,* by calling them *the very thing in all the world they are not:* old coats. (p. 133)

Tobacco Road attracted record audiences during the darkest years of the nation's history by working, largely through happy accident, this very *downward conversion* of the culture's anxieties into "old coats." Throughout the play, the dreaded scenes of poverty and dehumanization that haunted the people of the depression were invoked, and then pressed to the point of absurdity. The very real fears were thus misnamed as silliness and folly. Moreover, like the child who is made to see the demon as an old coat, the audience dissolved into giggles. This process can be illustrated by a few key scenes.

The opening scene presents a nightmare vision of family life, a worst-case scenario of the destruction of any sense of parental respect or familial affection under the debilitating weight of poverty. Dude stands throwing an old ball against the wall of the family home, manifesting a stupid disdain for Jeeter's requests that he stop before he breaks off any more of the siding. It is a horrifying scene; father and son are seemingly drained of human concern. Then Grandma enters. Hunched over, dirty, unspeaking, she shuffles near the house. As she does so, Dude begins throwing the ball at her "hard as he can," deliberately aiming it near her head with each throw, retrieving the ball, then throwing again. Grandma scampers and crawls under the porch. In a few seconds, the scene has been converted from horror to the ridiculous. Dude's cruelty is so exaggerated and, in this instant, his utter indifference to conventional moral behavior is so capsulized, that the scene becomes a moment of grotesque humor.

The play works this same conversion repeatedly. The horror scene of the Lesters' hunger becomes slapstick as Jeeter steals the sack of turnips while Lov is distracted by the sexual attractions of Ellie Mae. Similarly, the issue of child marriage – a common theme in 1930s sociological studies of the South – turns to comic treatment as Dude and Bessie become a bizarre, inverted version of the dreaded myth, carrying in bit by damaged bit the exploded symbol of American bourgeois life – their new automobile.

The most devastating of the downward conversions in *Tobacco Road* occurs in the final scene. Ada has been run over by Dude and Bessie's automobile and crawls on stage for her final moments of life. It is a dreadful, depressing scene. This woman, the mother of seventeen children, who has slaved away in abject misery for her entire life, now is to die in the dirt amid the complete indifference of her family, none of whom will even promise that she might be buried in a "fancy dress." The one child she cares about is being held by the wrist at the moment by Jeeter, who intends to force her into child marriage. Then, as her final act, Ada asks Jeeter to come nearer with Pearl and, as he does so, bites his arm; howling in pain, he lets go of Pearl. The child runs away, and Ada – having won this puny victory – dies. Ada is a kind of icon of suffering in the

play and, in this scene, her most pathetic moment is converted to hilarity with this farcical incident. The very real myth of
the suffering of poor women is converted to a moment of slapstick.

The most notorious conversions of the play have to do with
sexual behavior. American bourgeois culture, always suspicious
of the sexual mores of the lower classes, had developed elaborate myths about the "animalistic" behavior to which people
were reduced when living in poverty. These images found expression in the art of the period and – quite in keeping with
their predecessors in European models like Zola, Tolstoy, and
even Dickens – they portrayed the poor as oblivious to "higher" moral sensibilities. These grim naturalistic works, by writers like Grace Lumpkin and James Farrell, were augmented in
their mythmaking by the loose brand of anecdotal "sociological" study that flourished at this time. Images of sexual "depravity" came to take on a new level of threat as the depression
deepened and ever greater numbers of people saw themselves
as approaching the gaping maw of poverty. Suddenly, many
Americans who had always been middle class and those who
had struggled into that atmosphere during the boom years of
the twenties were faced with the prospect of becoming part of
the economic class they had scorned. People shuddered to hear
that seven of ten interviewees in the Lynds' Middletown study
reported having engaged in premarital sex.[19] The notions of
animal sexuality that the middle class associated with crushing
poverty threatened as a dark and imminent menace.

The culture of the thirties took action to protect the "standards of decency" that, in the popular mind, set middle-class
people apart from the poor. In a kind of preemptive strike
against a vague threat of dehumanization, doubtless made all

the more threatening as the images of "animalistic" sex carried with them considerable excitement, bourgeois culture launched a fresh campaign against what it perceived as laxness in sexual morality. They might be reduced in their incomes, people seemed to reason, but they would hang onto the principles of "decent behavior" that distinguished them from their inferiors. Within a few years' time in the early thirties, the *New York Times* protested against "almost naked people on the beaches," a teenage girl in Alhambra, California, won massive public support in a lawsuit she filed to avoid being forced to undress in a school locker room, and a huge letter-writing campaign helped to convince a judge to remove Bertrand Russell from his chair in Philosophy at City College of New York. A New York Supreme Court judge agreed with a plaintiff in the case that Russell's books were "lecherous, salacious, libidinous, lustful, venereous, erotomaniac, aphrodisiac, atheistic, irreverent, untruthful, bereft of moral fiber," and "narrow-minded."[20]

The stage production of *Tobacco Road* provided one of Burke's secular exorcisms of the images of sexual degradation that haunted bourgeois America in the depression. At the same time, it provided a lot of sexual excitement. By invoking these images of "animal" sexuality in exhibitions that were grotesquely exaggerated and that veered energetically into comedy, the play worked a powerful social therapy for the 1930s: It made sex fun. Dark and depressing sexual myths were enacted in the play, and then exploded into comedy (Figure 14). Audiences left feeling a weight of guilt and apprehension had been removed. The horrible thing that they feared had been renamed as something ridiculous.

Take, for example, the sexual behavior of Ellie Mae. This character represents a kind of bourgeois nightmare of unfet-

tered sexual desire. Because her harelip makes her unattractive
to men, Ellie Mae has no outlet for her drives and so is reduced
to the outright physical seduction of Lov, her sister's husband,
in the front yard, and in front of her entire family. She is described as "wriggling" across the dirt-covered stage, rubbing
her sex parts against the ground like a dog in heat, and – when
she reaches Lov – their "rubbing" up and down against one another is the acting out of a nightmare scene of unspeaking humans reduced to an "animal" sexuality. Then the scene dissolves into slapstick, quite literally: Jeeter takes off with the bag
of turnips that Lov left on the ground, Lov jumps up to yell
after him, and the women begin to beat him with sticks.

The same mechanism of downward conversion comes into
play in the other sexually charged scenes of the play. The public seduction of a teenage boy by a middle-aged female preach-
er turns comic, first by the absurdity of Dude's stupid grinning
and giggling, and then – when their "marriage" is consummat-
ed – by the ridiculous image of the rest of the family jockeying
for positions at the cabin windows to watch the action. The situation of Sister Bessie and Dude in bed is rendered even more
comic when Ada warns Bessie that she will have to make Dude
wear his socks in bed, as he never washes his feet. Through this
strategy of conversion, the play managed to be both sexually
exciting, in the voyeuristic pleasure it offered, as well as highly therapeutic in relieving bourgeois culture of a kind of sexual dread.

This "camping-up" of sex is symptomatic of the way the
play "worked," both as a piece of profitable theatre and as a
massively popular cultural icon. Sexual immorality was only
one of the things burlesqued by the play; the piece did the
same work of objectification and comic exaggeration upon the

Figure 14. Sex sells: Ruth Hunter (Ellie Mae) and Dean Jagger (Lov) in *Tobacco Road* (1933). (New York Public Library)

essential images of poverty, suffering, and dehumanization that
people of the 1930s saw wherever they looked: in newspapers,
newsreels, WPA photographs, in the title page of their theatre
program. People also heard news of suffering and degradation,
not only in radio reports of "conditions," but also in the ubiq-
uitous web of dire rumor and societal myth that permeates a
culture experiencing economic hardship. The stage production
of *Tobacco Road* brought representative images of all of those
cultural fears of suffering, debasement, and deprivation together in one potent package and pushed the images to the level of a cartoon. The resulting spectacle was an unintentional
piece of social therapy, a burlesque of suffering that placed
people's fears of sudden impoverishment and the collapse of
civilization in the context of extreme comedy, "out there," absurd, and considerably less potent, a protracted "skit" on a
compendium of horrors. The play remained popular and profitable as long as those anxieties dominated the national consciousness; then, beginning in 1942, they were gradually sup-
planted as the nation was swept up by both the practical and
ideological demands of world war and an economy that suddenly boomed in a rush of war production.[21] With surprising
swiftness, the play's popularity ebbed. The exaggerated images
of *Tobacco Road* no longer matched a dominant theme in the
national consciousness; it was anachronistic and its therapy no
longer meaningful or effective.

Tobacco Road and Satire

By saying that *Tobacco Road* was an unintentional burlesque,
I mean that Caldwell and Kirkland happened onto this effec-

tive formula by accident. Topical burlesques in the tradition of
Tom Thumb were, of course, prominent in the period. Pieces
like the hugely successful *Pins and Needles* (1936–40) and the
satirical musicals *Of Thee I Sing* (1931), *Let 'Em Eat Cake* (1933),
The Band Wagon (1931), *As Thousands Cheer* (1933), *Parade*
(1935), *I'd Rather Be Right* (1937), *Hooray for What!* (1937), and
Sing Out the News (1938) punctured politicians and political
rhetoric about issues of the day through techniques of mockery
and caricature, the same, often grotesque devices that have appeared in satire throughout history.

Tobacco Road was unique, however, in that its production
did not provide the ordering frame, the label "satire" or "review," that defined those other productions.[22] Because it also
invoked the grim images of naturalism in addition to exploding
them, the play retained a powerful ambivalence toward its subjects. The production thus remained ambivalent itself and was
open to the wide range of interpretations given it. Many intellectuals preferred to emphasize the social activism of the work,
and their perspective was not baseless. The massive popularity
of the play led to a congressional investigation of conditions in
the rural South and was often credited with prompting the laws
enacted during the depression to improve the credit status of
tenant farmers. The production was enough of a social drama
and enough of a comedy that its producers could feature Mrs.
Roosevelt's endorsement of it as "a play for sober-minded people interested in better social conditions" and the phrase "laugh
riot" on the same piece of advertising.[23] *Tobacco Road* offered
a kind of deflation that sneaked up on the audience; thoroughly mixed up in a complex confusion of signs, the cartooning of
the play left people with a satisfaction that was unrivaled by
any other piece of live theatre in the depression years.

The Film

The level of cultural threat in the play can be appreciated by taking a look at the Hollywood film that was made from it and the neutralizing bath through which the narrative was put when converted to an article of mass art. Caldwell and Kirkland sold the film rights for the play and novel versions of *Tobacco Road* to Darryl F. Zanuck; the project went into production at Twentieth Century–Fox in 1940 and was released early in 1941.[24] The film was written by Nunnally Johnson and directed by John Ford – the same team that had won praise from the Left in 1940 for *The Grapes of Wrath*. The record of Johnson's "conferences" with Zanuck tells a story of the elimination of the last traces of the grotesque from Johnson's already innocuous script. In at least twenty instances, Zanuck marked lines or incidents as "censorable" (in reference to the Hays Code) and insisted in conferences that Johnson delete or alter these passages. Not only were specific words or phrases deemed objectionable, but also whole story elements had to be neutralized. For example, Dude could not even talk about stealing; Jeeter could not suggest to Lov that he take Ellie Mae home to replace Pearl but only "to sort of take care of the place and cook for [him]"; and, in order to preserve the prohibition against mockery of ministers, Sister Bessie could not be allowed to sing hymns; Zanuck ordered that Johnson find "some other songs."[25]

The essential action of the "adaptation" from stage to film was to convert a play that shocked its audience through grotesque combinations of cartoon sex and social conscience into a sentimental, bucolic comedy about a family of lovable but stupid hicks. The sexual extremity and violence of the play and novel were removed, and the narrative was given an "up-beat"

Hollywood ending. Here are the most arresting of the film's in-
novations:

1. *Ellie Mae no longer has a harelip.* The character, portrayed
by Gene Tierney, is fetchingly smudged with dirt and attired
in a close-fitting dress, carefully ripped at the breast and thigh.
The effect is to create a fantasy of a tarnished beauty – a sort
of Cinderella – who, with a few moments of washing up, could
be transformed into her true and ravishing self. This version
of the character is fitting with the fantastic, sentimental nature
of the film as a whole, but – of course – makes complete nonsense of the fact that Ellie Mae is still unwed and desperate
for a husband. Her transformation is a sign for the transformation of the whole work: The beast has become a dusty beauty.

2. *The character of Pearl does not appear in the film.* The pursuit of Pearl by Lov – central to the plot of the play – is reduced to a marginal concern here. The film veers away from
the sexual issues at the heart of the play and focuses on a sentimental depiction of Jeeter (played by the comic actor Charlie
Grapewin) and his quaint attempts to raise money to save the
farm.

3. *The narrative is altered to provide a happy ending.* Whereas the play and novel end quite hopelessly – with Ada dead and
eviction imminent – the lovable Lesters of the film are saved
from destruction by a sentimental capriciousness on the part of
their landlord, Captain Tim. Jeeter and Ada, having failed to
raise money during a quaintly comic mission to town, have left
the farm and are walking to the county "poor farm." Ada, rather than dying under the wheels of a car, is marching at a good
clip along the road while a series of dolly shots follow a limp-
ing and pathetic Jeeter. A car slows and the driver offers them
a ride. It is Captain Tim himself who offers to drive them to

the poor farm. Jeeter drifts off to sleep and – when he awakes – finds that Captain Tim has driven them, not to the poor farm at all, but to their old home place! It will be no poor farm for them, Tim tells the Lesters, because he just came from town where he paid Jeeter's rent for a year. What's more, he gives Jeeter ten dollars to buy seed so that he can plant a crop and save the place permanently. Jeeter vows that he will go out soon and plow the fields and then, following a leitmotif set up in the rest of the film, yawns and settles down for a nap.

The transformation of *Tobacco Road* into the world of Hollywood cinema reminds us again of Adorno's accuracy in his analysis of the "consciousness industry" and its commodification of art, and of the relative freedom that the theatre enjoyed from this kind of industrial control. I do not mean to imply here that the "de-grotesquing" of *Tobacco Road* was the conscious work of any class or group of people in Hollywood studios, sitting around a boardroom table, their calendars marked: "Tuesday – Commodification meeting, 9 A.M.; Lunch with L.B. – Narcotization of the masses." However, the unconscious structures of ideology enforcement at work in the industry, powered by the overarching tectonics of the Hays Code (enacted by individuals subject to their own deviations and inconsistencies) were remarkably efficient in eliminating every disturbing element from *Tobacco Road*. The transformation by "the industry" was not simply a matter of toning down sexual content or altering an ending; rather, it meant the complete retooling of what had been an aesthetically messy, baroque work into a unified, streamlined product.

Tobacco Road, the film, is not a burlesque. The comic life of the narrative has been quite altered and the audience contract shifted so that the extremity, the symbolic potency of the play, has been eliminated. Instead of being pushed toward an attitude of ridicule, the audience is led, through sentimental devices, to identify with a cast of quaint country folk.[26] Moreover, in spite of the superficial restrictions of the Hays Code, the sex in the film – far from the objectifying incongruity of the play – is involving and seductive. Ford draws the viewer into the film product; his photography of Gene Tierney as El-lie Mae exhibits a textbook case of the exploitation of woman for visual pleasure outlined by Laura Mulvey.[27] Through these strategies of sentimental identification, exploitation, and closure, the "mind" of the film is aligned with attitudes that its presumed audience already held; the disruptive power of the play is ejected in the attempt of a hierarchical industry to create a palatable product. The strategy failed; the devices that the producers used to ingratiate the film to its audience served instead to remove what was the very source of the narrative's attractiveness, the guts of its cultural work: the therapeutic burlesque of impoverished suffering. The most profitable play of the decade was a financial flop as a Hollywood film.

Was the "satisfaction" offered by the stage production of *Tobacco Road* of a completely different order from the kind offered by this Hollywood precursor to *The Beverly Hillbillies?* Or was the play an example of what the Frankfurt School calls a "cultural drug," a work that soothed the fears of the population and thereby eased their impulses toward opposition, its authors unwitting assistants to hegemony?

The stage production of *Tobacco Road* offers a clear example of the double-edged quality of the grotesque – it "renamed" a cluster of cultural nightmares, thus providing distance and relief; but at the same time, it disrupted the status quo of which those nightmares were a part. By "curing" its audience of specific fears, *Tobacco Road* upset the hegemony that sentiment buttresses. Like the family of an alcoholic who stops drinking, the dominant ideology is disrupted and resentful when a part of its familiar structure is removed. The fears of sudden impoverishment and of reduction to "animal" sexuality were part of a systematic code of enforcement, part of a bourgeois ideological structure designed to preserve conservative codes of behavior. By withholding a sentimental closure – the play ends as pathetic and hopeless as it began – and by pulling people out of these middle-class anxieties, the play served a liberating function. The resistance to this liberation was manifested in the widespread "moral" attacks on the play and the hundreds of attempts to prevent its opening across the country. Dominant culture prefers that demons remain demons, when demons are part of the cultural works.

4

Chaos and Cruelty in the Theatrical Space
Horse Eats Hat, Hellzapoppin, and the Pleasure of Farce

Swing music is dangerously hypnotic. [It] is cunningly devised to a faster tempo than the human pulse and tends to break down conventions.

> –Psychologist to *The New York Times*, 1936

"The Dipsy Doodle," "Tutti Frutti," "Flat Foot Floogie with a Floy Floy"

> – Three of the top hit songs of 1937

FIBBER: Gosh darn it, I'll fix it myself. Where's my hammer? Oh, it's in the closet.

MOLLY: *(in alarm)* Don't open that door, McGee!

> – From *Fibber McGee and Molly*, radio's most popular program for much of the thirties

Hurry, please. The world is coming to an end and I have a lot to do.

> – New York woman to bus station operator upon hearing Orson Welles's *War of the Worlds* broadcast, 29 October 1938.[1]

IN 1931, ROBERT E. SHERWOOD proclaimed that depression culture was rich with evidence of the "anarchistic impulse . . . to be drunk and disorderly, to smash laws and ikons." For him, this turn toward anarchy was a manifestation of people's desperate desire to express their individuality in the face of a "revealed future" of totalitarian government, enforced uniformity, and the technological manipulation of human reproduction and thought.[2] Certainly the combined factors of economic collapse, threatening world war, the rise of dictatorships, and the rapid encroachment of technology into everyday life spawned in many the dark dread that civilization as they knew it was approaching its "end times." Every day the newspaper seemed to bring word of new international and domestic disasters: invasions in Europe and East Asia, rampant unemployment, violent strikes, kidnappings, and the notorious exploits of organized crime. Even nature seemed out of balance, as a devastating drought lingered in the Midwest and Plains and a hurricane of unprecedented violence killed thousands in Rhode Island and Connecticut. "What a hell of a time we are facing," Faulkner wrote to a friend. The world that would be left, he wrote, "would certainly not be worth living for." Still, he had a great desire to keep working, "to scratch the face of the supreme Obliteration and leave a decipherable scar of some sort."[3]

The grotesque inevitably comes into play when artists engage in the oxymoronic feat of giving "form" to "anarchy." Faulkner's own work of the depression is full of examples of desecration, of the "smashing of ikons": the calamitous gangster funeral in *Sanctuary,* in which the coffin spills its contents onto the floor amid a general melee; the ridiculous, multivalent appearances of the Snopes family in every nook and cranny of small-town life in *The Hamlet;* the convict's absurd adventures floating atop assorted buildings in the flood of *The Wild Palms.* In every case, this attempt to depict chaos took the form of farce.

The Danger of Farce

Eric Bentley has pointed out the vast possibilities of farce to enact aggression against convention, calling farce "a veritable structure of absurdities."[4] With its rapid pace and surprising turnabouts, farce has the greatest potential of any form to "capture" chaos in an aesthetic object. Farce opens the door to the grotesque when it places characters in perilous situations (threatened with discovery, injury, or even death) that exist in the context of a ridiculous world. Thus, farce leads the audience to laugh at the character's persistent misfortunes and suffering, the comic life preserved by the peculiar dreamlike quality of the action. This "dream contract" allows the audience to laugh at events that, were they to occur in a melodrama, would provoke empathy and commiseration. "Farce deals with the unreal," writes Albert Bermel, "with the worst one can dream or dread. Farce is cruel, often brutal, even murderous."[5] To be sure, the popularity achieved by farce in the depression was not a novel phenomenon. Farces had proven themselves to be money-makers throughout the history of the American theatre. Plays like *Up in Mabel's Room* and the record-setting *Abie's Irish Rose* were reliable fixtures of the American commercial stage of the 1920s, a decade that also witnessed the rise of the Marx Bros., George S. Kaufman, and Mae West as theatrical sensations. The thirties saw a continuation of the tradition, as plays like *Three Men on a Horse* (1935–8), *Boy Meets Girl* (1935–8), *Separate Rooms* (1940–3), *Brother Rat* (1936–9), *What a Life!*

(1938–41), and *Room Service* (1937–9) were among the seventeen productions of any kind that ran on Broadway for over five hundred performances. These plays – all of them George Abbott products except *Separate Rooms* – exhibited the breakneck pace, improbable narratives, and pressing circumstances that we associate with farce. The physical and verbal attacks upon authority figures that the protagonists are allowed to enjoy in these plays certainly offered depression audiences considerable Freudian pleasure and contributed to making farce the leading form in the commerical theatre. Still, these plays were mild in their effects when compared with two others from the period, productions that tapped an energy peculiar to the American scene in the 1930s.

Orson Welles's production of *Horse Eats Hat* and the Olsen and Johnson "scream-lined revue" *Hellzapoppin* exceeded the traditional boundaries of farce by raising the level of danger in the performance to new heights and by extending the disorder of the narrative into the audience's half of the theatre space. These violations of convention enhanced the antic release typical of farce, producing performances variously described as "mad," "chaotic," and "orgiastic." The levels of frenzy and release in these performances corresponded to the high level of cultural tension in the 1930s. These performances exploited and then surpassed the conventions of farce, becoming powerful enactments of the "anarchistic impulse" and making the farces of Abbott and Kaufman look tame and literary by comparison.

Welles Meets Labiche

Horse Eats Hat did not achieve the kind of long run enjoyed by the other plays mentioned here. It opened as the first production of Orson Welles's and John Houseman's WPA "Project

891" in late September 1936 and ran for only sixty-one performances. Nonetheless, the production did have a cult following
among certain segments of the population. On the evening of
its closing, only persons who had seen the production at least
twice were allowed to enter, and the audience was said to include a number of people who had seen the production as many
as twenty times.[6] Though the later performances are described
as festive occasions of much cheering and hilarity, the audience
response in the initial weeks was said to be more silent shock
than amusement. Marc Connelly described one performance
in which he and John Dos Passos "screamed with laughter"
throughout the evening while the rest of the audience sat in
a state of "general apathy."[7] Richard Watts of the *Herald Tribune* was not alone in giving the play a negative review at its
opening. He described feeling "that dismal embarrassment
which comes to one when actors are indulging in a grim determination to be high-spirited and there is nothing to be high-
spirited about."[8]

The audience's alienation in the early performances can be
explained by the machinelike quality that Welles instilled in the
production. As in his other work for the theatre, he directed
the play as a puppeteer, moving actors and scenery around the
stage and auditorium with a mechanical adroitness. The script
was developed by Welles with the translator Edwin Denby
from Eugène Labiche and Marc Michel's *Un chapeau de paille
d'Italie* (*The Italian Straw Hat*, 1851). Though Welles maintained the basic plot and comic tensions of the original play
(near-discoveries, mistaken identities, disguise), his version
contained fewer scenes, focusing the action more tightly on the
central character (Freddie) in his single-minded pursuit of a
hat and leaving the audience to fill in many gaps in the narrative. The adaptation selected only those scenes essential to the

one comic action, beginning by dramatizing the scene of the horse eating the hat (which had been related through dialogue in the original) and ending with the frantic celebration of the wedding party when an identical hat had been found. While the overall action was simpler than in *Un chapeau . . .* , Welles expanded the comic life of the scenes, drawing them out in length and interjecting metatheatrical elements into them. Freddie not only has to find a certain hat somewhere in Paris, while being closely pursued by his wedding party, but also has to cope with the fact that he is acting in a complicated play in which things keep going wrong, and in which fellow characters wander into the "other world" of the auditorium.

Throughout its length, the new version displayed Welles's attraction to a literal enactment of a Bergsonian notion of humor. Welles consistently constructed scenes in which characters behave like mechanical toys, their energies wound up and then released. In one scene, the hero is attempting to explain to his fiancée why he must, for the protection of a married woman's reputation, find a particular kind of woman's hat:

TILLIE: Freddie, if you ever lie to me, there is nothing I wouldn't stop at. NOTHING! I might act pretty rash.

> (SHE *slaps him on L. cheek,* HE *turns head front slowly.* FREDDIE *slaps her on L. cheek, and* SHE *turns front slowly. Arm in arm* THEY *walk down and stop in front of chairs. Pause, then slap* EACH OTHER.)

Now sit down and tell me all about it.[9]

In other scenes, characters are described as taking "3 large steps" or two characters in tandem are directed to take a "step R." after each line (p. II-19). Freddie and Gustave engage in a protracted "contest" of heel-clicking and bowing (p. III-3). Lat-

er, Gustave "responds to each phrase with an Oh, each growing in intensity and the last one continues into a laugh" (p. III-
4). Other characters are described as holding their hands in
specific positions, jumping backward before speaking each word
in a phrase, suddenly choking one another, or entering in the
"wrong" scene and being directed by the "prompter" to "GET
OUT!" (III-4–14). In the last instance, Welles adds to the joke
of this revelation of the theatre machine by having Freddie,
now uncertain of what to say next as this scene from his life has
been disrupted, turn front and shout the old vaudeville line,
"Save the furniture! . . . Save the furniture!" The "prompter"
restores the mechanical works by feeding Freddie his cue (III-
14). Similar metatheatrical jokes occur when scenery falls to re-
veal seemingly surprised actors in little clothing or in various
compromising positions.[10]

The machinelike functioning of the production reached its
peak in the last scene of Act III, a scene that John Houseman
described as "one of the most extravagant accumulations of farcical horror ever assembled behind the proscenium arch of a re-
spectable American theatre – not excluding *Hellzapoppin*."[11]
He found it so uncomfortable to watch the scene that he usually left the theatre just before it reached its climax:

I can still see Joe Cotten, wearing his bright yellow leather gloves,
with the coveted straw hat grasped firmly between his teeth, caught
between the Countess' indignant guests [each of whom produced
and began to fire a pistol] and the vengeful pursuit of the wedding
party, leaping from sofa to table to chandelier which, at that instant,
started to rise like a great golden bird, carrying him upward into a
wild, forty-foot flight into the fly-loft, while a three-tiered fountain
flung a giant jet upward at the seat of his pants and Cotten himself,
clinging to the rising chandelier with one hand and grasping a siphon

in the other, squirted streams of soda water over the madly whirling crowds below. As he rose, scenery moved erratically up and down; props seized with a sudden life of their own, were seen to fly off suddenly in various directions and a huge "Paris-by-night" backdrop came crashing down onto the stage floor, narrowly missing a platoon of stagehands – one of them in red flannel underwear – who had chosen this moment to carry a thirty-two foot ladder slowly, horizontally and imperturbably across the stage.

Just after this frantic scene (Figure 15), before the audience could leave the theatre for intermission, a woman dressed as a hussar appeared in the right mezzanine box and played two trumpet solos. During the applause for her performance, a player piano began to play "Sweet Rosie O'Grady" in the left upper box as a drunken member of the wedding party stumbled into view. Feeling trapped in the box, he climbed over the railing,

then, with a great cry, he slipped and fell and remained hanging, head down, with one foot caught in the railing, swinging like an erratic pendulum over the heads of the audience while the mechanical piano switched to Liszt's Hungarian Rhapsody No. 2.

Houseman's anxieties about this part of the performance must have seemed validated when, late in the run, the actor slipped while climbing over the railing, fell into the auditorium, and broke his leg in several places.[12]

It is unlikely that the attacks on the production by the Hearst newspapers were in response only to the rather tame sexual references it contained or to the expense of so massive a government-financed production. In addition to these more obvious factors, there is the question of the play's psychic liberation of its audience. Welles's production was a battering ram

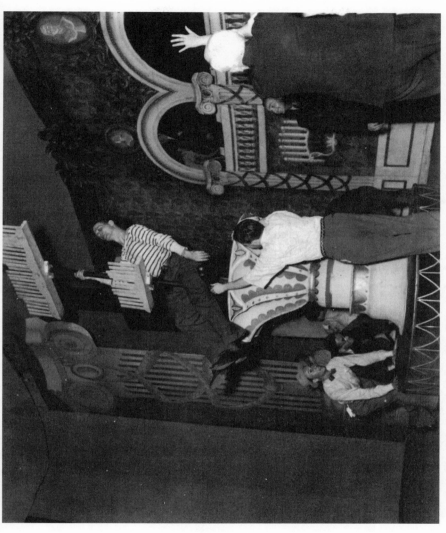

Figure 15. Joseph Cotten rehearses his ascent into the flies for the Labiche/Welles/Denby *Horse Eats Hat* (1937). (New York Public Library)

for smashing through conventions both social and aesthetic. It did the usual job of farce in "desecrating the household gods"[13] of marriage, respect for parents, respect for the law, and then went on to bring desecration to the subject of performance itself. The production showed an undeniable extravagance in threatening the audience, first by pulling down the conventions of performance at will (the falling scenery, the fake miscues) and then by placing actors in positions of actual physical peril.

John Houseman's impulse to leave the theatre before the dangerous scene of Joseph Cotten's sudden flight into the loft and Bil Baird's suspension from the railing of the upper box was likely shared by many in the audience. Not only is there actual danger in staging such scenes, no matter how well rehearsed they may be, but also Welles deliberately constructed these moments to make them *look* as dangerous as they were. In the flying scene, the sudden, chaotic changing of scenery and the introduction of the ladder-bearing stagehand into the theatrical world creates a feeling of disorder in the performance itself, urging the spectator to engage in the thought that *something has gone wrong*. At the same time, one would tell oneself that "It's all part of the play," but the doubt has been firmly planted, and the tension would not be relieved until the scene had ended. However, it was not clear when the scene was over; Welles kept prolonging the tension. Richard France, who interviewed Welles, Houseman, and actors involved in the production, reconstructed the moment after Cotten's ascent:

The entire scene becomes chaotic; even the setting seems to be out of control. Back drapes go up. The front curtain tumbles to the floor. Prop men pick their way through the debris trying to save what they can. . . . Finally six butlers in livery pick their way to the footlights and announce, "Supper is served!" The curtain falls.[14]

But the scene is still not over. As the houselights go on, the trumpeter begins her playing, followed by the piano and the metatheatrical episode of the drunken guest. The act was not really over until Baird had completed his "controlled fall" onto a mattress in the orchestra pit and the audience could make its way safely into the lobby.

My point here is that Welles's accentuation of both the machinery of the theatre and the physical endangerment of the actors contributed to a shattering, thrilling theatrical event that provided some of its audience members a secret, terrible pleasure. Like spectators at an auto race or a tightrope exhibition, they were allowed to enjoy seeing another person in a situation of grave risk. The "teasing" in which Welles engaged by exposing the workings of the theatre machine heightened this experience by removing from it some of the security one feels in the safety of a performance. Those repeated metatheatrical jokes prevented people from saying to themselves with complete confidence, "It's all part of the play." Welles presented a theatre machine in which things seem to go wrong, in which the machine itself at times seemed to seize the controls, in which human beings had but an insecure charge of the theatrical world. The result was a theatre piece that offered the pleasure of extreme violations, that toyed not just with the usual "pretend" danger of the discovery of an amorous couple by a jealous husband, but with the physical safety of the actors themselves in a mad, irrational world. Those who found the play hilarious, who joined into this unusually dangerous festival spirit, were enjoying the explosion of reality's rules – a comic apocalypse, a taunting of physics, phenomenology, and the oppressive logic of history. Here, the seeming inevitability of civilization's doom, the pressing relationship of events and their consequences, of economic disaster and war, were suspended and ridiculed. One "world" could at any moment collapse and show itself to be a sham constructed by another "world." The audience could enjoy a vicarious liberation from the pressures of the age through the magical possibilities of Welles's well-timed fate machine, a psychic participation in the hero's escape from the mob on a cooperative and flying chandelier.

The question must inevitably arise as to why, if *Horse Eats Hat* was so powerful in its effects, it left many audience members cold and distinctly unconvulsed. Connelly described these people as "watching it, rather than sharing in it"; they seemed, he said, "not attuned to the play."[15] In many ways, the production was typical of pieces that have tended to attract "cult" rather than "mass" audiences. Like *The Rocky Horror Picture Show* or the plays of Charles Ludlam, the production plied a brand of the grotesque that appealed to a passionate minority with specific sensitivities. The consistent attack of *Horse Eats Hat* – the destruction of the image of the theatre as metaphor for a rational world – seems to have been especially attractive to artists and intellectuals. In addition to the story of Connelly and Dos Passos laughing "like hyenas" in the midst of a stone-faced audience, there is Martin Gabel's statement that "the fine arts world – the opera buffs and curators – many of them adored it." As in any manifestation of the grotesque, a portion of the audience was likely to have been merely puzzled or even bored by the spectacle. Like certain other twentieth-century examples of the grotesque composed by highly self-conscious artists – a Buñuel film, for example, or a Tzara poem – Welles's production did not prove accessible to a mass audience. The performance worked its particular liberation only for a coterie who were "attuned" to Welles's personal comic vision. The mass of theatregoers were left to seek escape in entertainments with lower thresholds and less paradoxical jokes.

Hellzapoppin

If Orson Welles experimented with extending the chaos of farce into the auditorium in *Horse Eats Hat*, Olsen and Johnson expanded and exploited this maneuver to its utmost in the massively popular *Hellzapoppin*. Here, the narrative pretense of a "revue" was constantly interrupted by staged incidents in the auditorium that included various forms of physical attacks on the audience. For three hours, the audience was tricked, showered with beans, blasted with air hoses, accosted by actors costumed as gorillas and clowns, fired upon with blank charges, and – finally – thrown out of the theatre by male and female "cleaning women." Olsen and Johnson pretended to struggle throughout the evening to get the revue back on track by moving from one "legitimate" vaudeville act to the next; but the hosts seemed to find themselves perpetually overwhelmed by insanity, their own and that of the multitude of audience "plants." Though most critics at its opening found *Hellzapoppin* to be excessively loud and vulgar (Burns Mantle called it "a noisy and irresponsible riot"), the show quickly began playing to near-capacity audiences in New York and in tours across the country. The production was a phenomenon of environmental absurdity that has not been repeated in the American commercial theatre.[16]

Hellzapoppin opened at the Forty-sixth Street Theatre in September 1938, but soon moved to the larger Winter Garden. The production was assembled by Ole Olsen and Chic Johnson, vaudeville "headliners" for over a quarter-century, who created the piece from gags they had used on a smaller scale for years in their tours on the fading vaudeville circuit. With the addition of original music by Sammy Fain and the insertion of a dozen "real" variety acts, Olsen and Johnson created a spectacle that ran on Broadway for 1,404 performances. During the New York run and as late as 1943, two touring companies played versions of the show in cities across the country, with Olsen and Johnson's roles taken first by Billy House and Eddie Garr (fresh from his performance as Jeeter Lester in *Tobacco Road*), and later by Lew Parker and a virtually unknown young comedian named Jackie Gleason.[17] After 1940, the show was called *The New Hellzapoppin*, but the framework and most of the gags remained the same. A largely unsuccessful attempt to adapt the "accidental" and metatheatrical effects of the live performance to the medium of film was produced by Mayfair and released by Universal Pictures in 1941.[18] Olsen and Johnson attempted to revive the show in London in 1948, but it ran for only a short time. Unblushing in their attempts to capitalize on their single Broadway success, Olsen and Johnson again "revived" the piece as part of a water show in Flushing Meadow, Queens, in 1959. The event was titled *Hellz-a-splashin': An Aqua-cade*.[19]

The original *Hellzapoppin* was by no means a traditional, by which I mean *narrative*, farce. Reviewers struggled to define a genre for the production, choosing words ranging from "musical comedy" to "vaudeville" and "circus." Brooks Atkinson avoided the problem altogether by warning in the opening line, "Folks, it's going to be a little difficult to describe this one" and then referring to the production throughout the review simply as "it."[20] The piece did, however, have much in common with farce, both in the loose narrative of two comics putting on a show that keeps getting out of control and in its characteristic effects of comic violence and desecration of moral and aesthetic conventions (Figure 16). Much of the evening was enveloped in the grotesque, as various acts of violence and mutilation were carried out with comic exuberance. Between the

Figure 16. From the strange cast of *Hellzapoppin* (1938) *(left to right):* Harry Rieso, George Mann, Peggy Baldwin, Dewey Barto, Happy Moore, and (held horizontally) Stormy Birch. (Shubert Archive)

"legitimate" acts (which included two vocal quartets, a magician, a comic dancer, and several large musical numbers with a female chorus), and often in competition with them, a large cast of "stooges" disrupted the "official" performance with their own, often violent, activities: A seemingly nude woman mounted on a white horse enters an upper box, proclaims herself to be Lady Godiva, and remains there, with the horse, throughout the performance; a man, who has been wandering the aisles calling out desperately for "Lena" is eventually shot by Olsen and his body dragged offstage; vendors move frequently through the auditorium selling snacks, balloons, razor blades; a man hawks tickets for *Abe Lincoln in Illinois*, a competing show on Broadway; during a total blackout, an amplified voice describes the millions of spiders and snakes that have escaped into the theatre; at the same time, technicians clad in black move through the theatre, tossing small beans down people's necks, shooting compressed air at their feet, and tickling their heads and necks with stringy "teasers" on long poles (Figure 17); an actor dressed as a gorilla enters a box and removes a screaming young woman as her "date" cowers in fear; a woman in the orchestra section repeatedly shushes her screaming "baby" which, after a gunshot during a blackout, is heard no more; a "music lover" in the balcony repeatedly calls out for the orchestra to play his favorite pieces; "Lena" enters, wanders the aisles calling out for "Oscar," and, not finding him, commits suicide in the orchestra; actors shave, wash clothes, and make sounds on various unusual musical instruments from the boxes; a woman makes her way noisily from the middle of the orchestra section to the aisle and then announces that she is not leaving, but is only going to the "ladies room"; a silent and annoying clown, who has been wandering the aisles with

Figure 17. *Hellzapoppin*: The audience is blasted with air as a voice informs them that spiders have escaped into the theatre. (Shubert Archive)

a perpetual look of sadness and gloom, soliciting handouts and sympathy, is eventually placed in a cannon and seemingly fired through the roof; a delivery boy, who attempts throughout the performance to deliver to a "Mrs. Jones" a plant (Figure 18) that grows larger with each entrance, is found at the end of the performance seated in its branches in the lobby, still calling out for "Mrs. Jones" (Figure 19).[21]

The "official" performance itself was grotesque enough. The evening began with a "newsreel" featuring footage of Adolf Hitler, Mussolini, Winston Churchill, Roosevelt, and La Guardia, all of them speaking with incongruous ethnic accents and all in praise of the show that was about to begin; Hitler spoke with a thick Yiddish accent. After the entrance of Johnson and Olsen in a car pulling a trailer, an "escape artist" was introduced and, with a drum-roll accompaniment, he attempted to free himself from a straitjacket in the promised thirty seconds. Unable to do so, and growing ever more frantic, the man was dragged offstage, only to reappear – still struggling and flopping on the floor – at unexpected moments throughout the evening. "Barto and Mann" was a vaudeville team notable for the two men's great difference in height: Mann was over seven feet tall and Barto less than five. Part of their act consisted of an absurd "ballroom" dance, with Mann in "drag" throwing Barto around the stage and performing highly athletic leaps from off of the smaller man's bent leg.[22] In another sketch, Barto played a father attempting to discipline his enormous child, who continually pounded his father on the head. A later act featured a woman named Shirley Wayne, described by Atkinson as looking "as though she were just on the point of frying a mess of doughnuts," who played poorly on the violin. Near the end of the evening, after various musical acts and chorus numbers,

Olsen and Johnson held a "raffle" in which they gave away various large items to members of the audience: a six-foot wooden stepladder, a mop, a child's toilet chair, a twenty-five-pound bag of flour, a live chicken, a twenty-pound block of ice (Figure 20). Olsen and Johnson forced resistant audience members to accept the "prizes"; one moment featured in a magazine spread shows a man explaining that he doesn't need the ice because he has a refrigerator, while Johnson insists, "You'll take it and like it!"[23]

Hellzapoppin offered a superlative example of Bentley's notion of farce as "hostility enjoying itself."[24] Here, for a few hours, every violence was possible without risk. Beatings, murder, suicide, attacks on every kind of authority were carried out in a context of *fun*. The show's expression of hostility toward authority was not limited to the grotesque image/voice manipulations of the opening "newsreel." Olsen and Johnson brought the aggression into the theatre itself when they directed a comic anger toward the New York critics. On the opening night of *The New Hellzapoppin* in December 1939, the critics were singled out of the audience for abuse. As the evening progressed, they were the special targets for lobbed bananas, beans, and hard-boiled eggs; in addition, the "raffle" was rigged so that the critics were presented with all of the prizes. Olsen and Johnson wrote a special sketch for the occasion, in which actors portrayed the eight members of the New York Critics' Circle meeting to discuss their failure to close *Hellzapoppin* and so further their goal of a world with "no actors, no plays, no theatres; nothing but critics." At one moment in the short sketch, Arthur Pollock challenges the chair, John Anderson, and the exchange ends in a concise statement of Olsen and Johnson's explanation for the popularity of their show:

Figure 18. *Hellzapoppin*: The first of many attempts to deliver a plant. (Shubert Archive)

Figure 19. *Hellzapoppin:* As the audience leaves the theatre, the delivery man still calls out for "Mrs. Jones." The plant is now grown to the size of a tree. Meanwhile, Theodore Hardeen is still straitjacketed, the result of an earlier gag. (Shubert Archive)

POLLOCK: I saw *Hellzapoppin* and I thought it was kinda funny.

ANDERSON: *(bangs gavel on Pollock's hand; picks up seltzer bottle and squirts him in the face with it)* I suppose you think that's funny?

POLLOCK: Yes. It has an element of surprise.

ANDERSON: *(Picks up pie and socks Pollock in the face with it)* Do you mean to tell me this is funny?

POLLOCK: It's primitive, but there's a certain public demand for it.[25]

The "public demand" for the comic belittlement of authority was at the core of Olsen and Johnson's attacks on the critics. They defined the critics as representatives of "official" taste, and so the attacks on them became a part of the more general inversion of values.

When asked by a columnist to define what *Hellzapoppin* really was, Olsen responded,

What is it? Just a lot of fun. We think people want fun these days. No, we don't say it is necessarily comedy. It's fun when everybody has a part in it, when the audience feels that it is a part of the show. It's fun when you laugh with it. It's comedy when you laugh at it.[26]

What Olsen says about fun being the dominant mode of the show resonates with Bentley's idea of fun as the "ordering principle" of the universe of farce:

In farce chance ceases to seem chance, and mischief has method in its madness. One final effect of farce is that mischief, fun, misrule seem an equivalent of fate, a force not ourselves making, neither for righteousness nor for catastrophe, but for aggression without risk.[27]

Fun made *Hellzapoppin* the ultimate escapist theatre experience of the Great Depression. In a position of actual safety, its audiences could play at participating in every kind of dese-

Figure 20. *Hellzapoppin*: Chic Johnson forces an audience member to accept a "prize," which in this case was a t⌀   raining chair. If faced with resistance, Johnson would insist, "You'll take it and like i⌀

⌀rt Archive)

cration imaginable, and all of it controlled by a principle of fun
– and so beyond their personal or social responsibility. The
very title, *Hellzapoppin*, implied the temporary but unstop-
pable reign of a dark and mischievous force. Audiences, bom-
barded on every side by shocks and explosions, could experience the overturning of conventional notions of "the good"
without themselves taking on any guilt for the consequences.
Even Olsen and Johnson played at being innocent victims of
this invertive power, struggling to put on a "real" show but
finding disorder at every turn.

The creators of *Hellzapoppin* were conscious of the relation
of the production to the present moment, finding a correlation
between the seeming madness of the cultural moment and the
antic pleasures offered by the show. A letter from Olsen and
Johnson to the columnist John Anderson resembles nothing so
much as the manifestoes of the Dadaists in the teens, as they
urged a kind of art adequate to the terrific energies of their age:

Dear John Anderson::::
Bang! Bang! Bang!
Bang! Bang! Bang!
%$$"$$&!!!!
. . . Like you, we are slightly confused ourselves – what with Charlie McCarthys – Snow Whites and the Seven Dwarfs – Radio
singers being elected governors – guys crossing the Atlantic in $900
crates – Princeton defeated by Rutgers – LaFollette defeated in Wis-
consin – Welles scaring Hell out of the Country with a Bogey Man
Broadcast – and *Hellzapoppin* a Hit! We don't blame you for suggesting that the country is "NUTS."
– but THAT is the trend of our present National Emotional
Mood, and as has always been our theory: "Give the PUBLIC what
they THINK they want when they want it . . . !"
ANENT England and *Hellzapoppin*!!![28]

Olsen and Johnson were surely right in the connection they saw between the disorder of the moment and the "fixing" of disorder in *Hellzapoppin*. However, the salutary effect of the production had another, and more subtle, dimension as well: It offered a liberation from morality. The need for this kind of temporary escape from "goodness" was especially keen in the depression years. It was a time of great social consciousness; popular culture was filled with messages of social responsibility and personal integrity.[29] Virtually every mode of communication, from Roosevelt's speeches to Hollywood musicals, called for social discipline and self-sacrifice to face the desperate times. Roosevelt called for "social justice through social action" and asked Americans to hold themselves, each one, to demanding standards of courage, cooperation, and generosity. Popular culture echoed these social values. *How to Win Friends and Influence People* (1937) defined a new way for success: through cooperation rather than competition. Shirley Temple's perpetual screen self was persistently forced to suffer deprivation and heartbreak but eventually found happiness through her kindness to others. Dorothy Gale in *The Wizard of Oz* (1939) achieved her own wish, not by pursuing it at the expense of her fellows, but by sacrificing her own desires in order to help her friends; her reward was the discovery of the companionship and love she had been seeking from the start.

In the world of *Hellzapoppin*, Dorothy and Shirley would be revealed as sickening brats, and some comic disaster would certainly befall them. The show offered three hours of abandon, a vacation from depression demands on the audience member's social and personal conscience. The audience's secret, hostile desires were acted out among them and, through their laughter, they enjoyed a vicarious participation in the violence. Even the most horrible, demonic desires were enacted in the "safe inversion" of the world of *Hellzapoppin:* Here, annoying people met a violent end, the pious clown was fired through the roof, and someone finally shut up that squalling brat.

Farce and Containment

Artaud praised the early Marx Bros. films as "hymn[s] to anarchy and total rebellion,"[30] a statement that could as well be applied to *Horse Eats Hat* and *Hellzapoppin*. In fact, in their chaotic dramatic worlds, both plays bear certain resemblances to the work of the surrealists with whom Artaud had once associated himself. Still, though farce may be the most violent form of art, it is perhaps the least ideologically disruptive. By offering their audiences so much pleasure and release, these productions tended to dispel resentments, to some extent reconciling audiences to injustices that may have been represented in the course of the performances.

These productions are examples of the containment of the grotesque. Grotesque effects were employed throughout both productions, but – at least for those "attuned" to the performances – the disturbance provoked by these incongruities was dispelled through laughter. Artaud is right in calling farces hymns to anarchy and rebellion; they are enactments of social and moral revolutions, but the anarchy is contained within the performance and not carried into the street. Unlike the related form of melodrama, used to considerable effect in the thirties to "stir up" political *feeling* (Krutch came out of *Stevedore* "ready to crack someone over the head"), farce provides a personal liberation rather than a public disturbance.[31] Audiences who emerged from the theatre having laughed for three hours

at *Horse Eats Hat* or *Hellzapoppin* would have felt terrific, pos-
sessors of a new sense of freedom and even confidence in the
face of tremendous social doubt. They had joined in hymns to
anarchy, yes, but the theatre was for them as much a kind of
hospital as it was a kind of church.

Living with the Grotesque

With the attack on Pearl Harbor on 7 December 1941, the curtain came down on the period that Warren Susman called the
"Adlerian age of adjustment."[32] Driven by a new sense of national purpose and an economy newly booming with production of rubber, steel, textiles, and armaments, American culture
lurched out of Sherwood's "limbo-like interlude" and into a
new age that would bring unprecedented industrial growth and
the creation of a burgeoning, multifarious consumer culture.
For a few decades, at least, the country would have a clearer
idea of its own identity. With that greater clarity in the national "mentality," American culture no longer needed the particular species of the grotesque that had flourished in the crisis of
the depression. Popular preferences turned in the forties and
fifties to less contentious entertainments, whether strident and
discursive like the plays of Arthur Miller, delicate and pessimistic as in the work of Tennessee Williams, or saccharine and
fantastic like the sentimental dreams of American family life in
the television series of the 1950s. Mainstream Hollywood film
developed to extremity its already strong tendencies toward
sentiment (*Lassie Come Home*, 1943; *The Bells of St. Mary's*,
1945), the heroic (*The Ten Commandments*, 1957; *Ben-Hur*, 1959),
and to mythic presentations of the American West (*Shane*, 1953;

The Searchers, 1956). The celebrated horror films of the fifties tended to be parodies of their more disturbing depression originals (*I Was A Teenage Werewolf,* 1957) or part of the new breed of "paranoia" narratives reflecting the untempered fear of communist infiltrations (*Invasion of the Body Snatchers,* 1956; *I Married a Monster from Outer Space,* 1957). The grotesque continued as part of the cultural "show" of the forties and fifties, but in the context of the greater unanimity and purposiveness of these decades it was pushed from the central position that it had held during the depression.

Each cultural moment, it seems, develops grotesques that meet the specific needs of the time. In periods of great tension and confusion, like the Great Depression, these objects achieve a prominent position, appearing in a vast array of media, permeating the cultural fabric, animating art and entertainment both "high" and "low." In periods of relative stability and social confidence, grotesque objects are relegated to a subsidiary role within culture, correspondent in importance to the level of contradiction in the undercurrents that exist in even the most unified of cultures. In such periods of social cohesiveness, entertainments like the savage vaudeville forced upon Nathanael West's Lemuel Pitkin in *A Cool Million* or the cruel madness of *Hellzapoppin* are not part of the main cultural show, as they were in depression America. In more settled times, culture's monsters are left to perform in the shadows of the wings or in obscure side shows, and late, late at night.

Appendix
Cast and Staff Information
for Principal Productions

Arsenic and Old Lace

Opened 10 January 1941. A comedy in three acts by Joseph
Kesselring. Produced by Howard Lindsay and Russel Crouse
at the Fulton Theatre, New York. Directed by Bretaigne Windust. Scenery by Raymond Sovey.

Original cast:

Abby Brewster	Josephine Hull
Martha Brewster	Jean Adair
Teddy Brewster	John Alexander
Mortimer Brewster	Allyn Joslyn
Jonathan Brewster	Boris Karloff
Dr. Einstein	Edgar Stehli
Elaine Harper	Helen Brooks
The Rev. Dr. Harper	Wyrley Birch
Officer Brophy	John Quigg
Officer Klein	Bruce Gordon
Officer O'Hara	Anthony Ross

> Lieutenant Rooney . . . . Victor Sutherland
> Mr. Gibbs . . . . Henry Herbert
> Mr. Witherspoon . . . . William Parke

The production ran for a total of 1,444 performances. Among the substitutions later in the run were Bela Lugosi and then Erich von Stroheim as Jonathan Brewster. A London production opened at the Strand Theatre on 23 December 1942 and ran for 1,337 performances.

In June 1941, Warner Brothers purchased the rights to the play for $175,000. The screen version was released in September 1944, with a screenplay by Julius and Philip Epstein and directed by Frank Capra. The cast again featured Josephine Hull and Jean Adair as the elderly sisters, but with Cary Grant as Mortimer and Raymond Massey as Jonathan. Peter Lorre played Dr. Einstein.

End of Summer

Opened 17 February 1936 at the Guild Theatre, New York. A comedy in three acts by S. N. Behrman. Produced by the Theatre Guild, Inc. Directed by Philip Moeller. Scenery by Lee Simonson.

> *Original cast:*
> Leonie Frothingham . . . . Ina Claire
> Paula Frothingham . . . . Doris Dudley
> Sam Frothingham . . . . Minor Watson
> Mrs. Wyler . . . . Mildred Natwick
> Dr. Kenneth Rice . . . . Osgood Perkins
> Robert . . . . Kendall Clark
> Dennis McCarthy . . . . Van Heflin

Dr. Dexter . . . . Herbert Yost

Boris, Count Mirsky . . . . Tom Powers

The production ran for 152 performances.

Hellzapoppin

Opened 22 September 1938 at the 46th Street Theatre, New York. Produced by Ole Olsen and Chic Johnson in association with the Shubert organization and Harry Kaufman. A revue in two acts with music, conceived and written by Ole Olsen and Chic Johnson, with additional dialogue by Tom Mc-Knight. Most music by Sammy Fain and lyrics by Charles Tobias. Staged by Edward Duryea Dowling.

Original cast and episodes:
ACT I

1. Hellz-a-poppin (song & dance) . . . . Ensemble
2. Trans-continental (sketch) . . . . Olsen & Johnson
3. Fuddle Dee Duddle (song & dance) . . . . sung by
   Bonnie & Mel Reed, danced by Betty Mae &
   Beverly Crane and Ensemble
4. A Bedtime Story (sketch) . . . . Olsen & Johnson
5. Holmes and Hawkshaw (sketch)
   Inspector Guiness . . . . Ole Olsen
   Inspector Hennissey . . . . Chic Johnson
   Maid . . . . Mel Reed
   Mrs. Ifingprattle . . . . Dorothy Thomas
   Mr. Ifingprattle . . . . Eddie Bartell
   Gangster . . . . Walter Nilsson
   Murderer . . . . James Hollywood
   Salesman . . . . Sidney Gibson
   Meadows . . . . Sidney Chatton
6. Strolling Thru the Park (song & dance) . . . . Olsen &
   Johnson with female chorus

7. Walter Nilsson (unicyclist)
8. Before the Curtain . . . . Ole Olsen [then:]
   The Maternity Ward (sketch)
   Dr. Bringem . . . . Dewey Barto
   Lovejoy . . . . Bobby Barry
   The Baby . . . . George Mann
9. Before the Curtain . . . . Ole Olsen [then:]
   Wall Street (sketch)
   1st Victim . . . . Sidney Gibson
   2nd Victim . . . . Bobby Barry
   3rd Victim . . . . Hal Sherman
   4th Victim . . . . Happy Moore
10. Abe Lincoln (song) . . . . . . by Earl Robinson and Alfred
    Hayes, sung by The Charioteers
11. A Cabinet Meeting (sketch)
    Chancellor . . . . Ole Olsen
    Minister of War . . . . Sidney Dean
    Minister of Finance . . . . J. C. Olsen
    Minister of the Navy . . . . Henry Howe
    Secretary of Foreign Affairs . . . . John Callahan
    Minister of Propaganda . . . . Henry Howe
    Orderly . . . . James Hollywood
    An American . . . . Chic Johnson
12. Shaganola (song & dance) . . . . sung by Bonnie & Mel
    Reed, danced by Roberta and Ray
    and the Ensemble
13. The Radio Rogues (imitations) . . with Jimmy Hollywood,
    Eddie Bartell, Sidney Chatton
14. Who's the Dummy? (sketch) . . . . with Olsen & Johnson,
    Eddie Bartell, Sidney Chatton, Dorothy Thomas
15. Shirley Wayne (novelty music act) . . . .
16. Olsen and Johnson, assisted by Billy Adams . . . .
17. It's Time to Say Aloha (song) . . . sung by Cyrel Roodney
    and June Winters, danced by Ray
    Kinney and Aloha Maids and the Ensemble
    Lena (who looks for Oscar) . . . . Catherine Johnson

ACT II

1. Harem on the Loose (song)
2. The Magic Hour (sketch) . . . . with Olsen & Johnson
   and "Hardeen"
3. The Charioteers (quintet) . . . .William Williams, Edward
   Jackson, Ira Williams, Jimmy Sherman, Howard Daniels
4. Hal Sherman
5. Pep Talk . . . . from Ole Olsen
6. When You Look in Your Looking Glass (song) . . by Paul
   Mann and Steven Weiss, sung by Cyrel Roodney and
   June Winters, danced by Betty Mae & Beverly Crane
   and the Ensemble, specialty dance by Barto and Mann
7. Audience Participation . . . audience and Olsen & Johnson
   and cast
8. Finale – It's Time to Say Aloha (song & dance) . . . Olsen
   & Johnson, Barto & Mann, Hal Sherman, Radio Rogues,
   Theodore Hardeen, Reed Sisters, Betty Mae & Beverly Crane,
   Cyrel Roodney, June Winters, and Entire Ensemble

The Ensemble included the following:

The Misses – Phyllis McBride, Helen Felix, Claire Kaktin, Eve-
   lyn Deffon, Mary Barth, Dorothy Thomas, Peggy Regan,
   Virginia Collins, Sally Bond, Evelyn Albright, Kay Wilson,
   Margaret Bacon, Dawn Greenwood, Blanche Poston, Elaine
   Caruso, Naomi Libby, Madeline O'Hara, Karl Lynn, Phyl-
   lis Lake, Evelyn Laurie, Jean Beryl, Regina Lewis, Marjorie
   Conrad, Renee Havel, Margie Young
The Messrs. – Adolph Gudel, William Chandler, Philip Johnson,
   George Miller, Fuzzy Lentz, Frank Sheppard.

The show moved to the Winter Garden Theatre soon after
its opening, where it played for three years (a total of 1,404
performances). The show was revised in 1939 and part of that
run was under the title (beginning 11 December) *The New
Hellzapoppin*. The show toured successfully in the United
States in the 1940s. The first tour was headlined by Eddie

Garr and Billy House and the second tour by Jackie Gleason and Lew Parker.

A film version was released by Universal Pictures in December 1941. The film was described as being "suggested by the Olsen and Johnson stage play" but was given a plot, based on an original story by Nat Perrin and using a screenplay by Nat Perrin and Warren Wilson. The film was directed by H.C. Potter. Though it starred Olsen and Johnson, the film used almost no one else from the stage production.

Horse Eats Hat

Opened 26 September 1936 at the Maxine Elliot Theatre, New York. Presented by Project 891 of the Federal Theatre Project of the Works Progress Administration. A farce in five acts, by Edwin Denby and Orson Welles, based on *Un chapeau de paille d'Itallie* by Eugène Labiche and Marc Michel. Directed by Orson Welles. Costumes and scenery by Nat Karson. Lighting by Abe Feder. Original music by Paul Bowles, orchestrated by Virgil Thomson.

> *Original cast:*
> Freddy . . . . Joseph Cotten
> Mugglethorp . . . . Orson Welles
> Entwhistle . . . . George Duthie
> Uncle Adolphe . . . . Donald MacMillian
> Queeper . . . . Dana Stevens
> Bobbin . . . . Hiram Sherman
> Grimshot, Lieut. of Cavalry . . . . Sidney Smith
> Joseph . . . . Harry McKee
> Gustave, Viscount . . . . France Bendtsen
> Augustus . . . . Edgerton Paul

Myrtle Mugglethorp . . . . Virginia Welles
Agatha Entwhistle . . . . Paula Laurence
Tillie . . . . Arlene Francis
The Countess . . . . Sarah Burton
Daisy . . . . Henrietta Kay
Clotilda . . . . Lucy Rodriguez
Corporal . . . . Bernard Savage
Butler . . . . Walter Burton
First Footman . . . . Steven Carter
Second Footman . . . . J. Headley
Raguso . . . . Enrico Cellini
Berkowitz . . . . George Barter
Horse . . . . Carol King and Edwin Denby
At the Nickelodeon . . . . Edgerton Paul

Wedding Guests – Ellen Worth, Arabella St. James, Marie
Jones, Hattie Rappaport, Anna Gold, Myron Paulson, Wallace Axton, Pell Dentler, George Leach, Bil Baird

Tillie's Girls – Peggy Hartley, Terry Carlson, Lee Molnar,
Gloria Sheldon, Teresa Alvarez, Opal Essant, June Thorne,
Mildred Colt, Geraldine Law

Countess' Guests – Georgia Empry, Solomon Goldstein, May
Angela, Lawrence Hawley, Margaret Maley, Jack Smith,
Mary Kukavski, Elizabeth Malone, Helena Rapport, Helene
Korsun, Nina Salama, Julie Fassett, Jane Hale, Jane John-
son, Michael Callaghan, Don Harward, Walter LeRoy,
Harry Merchant, Warren Goddard

Citizens Night Patrol – Arthur Wood, James Perry, Victor
Wright, Robert Hopkins, Craig Gordon, Harry Singer,
Frank Kelly, Bernard Lewis, Henry Russele, Charles Uday,
George Smithfield, Henry Laird, Edwin Hemmer, George
Armstrong, Jerry Hitchcock, Tod Brown

The production ran for sixty-one performances.

Idiot's Delight

Opened 24 March 1936 at the Shubert Theatre, New York. Produced by the Theatre Guild, Inc. A play in three acts by Robert E. Sherwood. Staged by Bretaigne Windust. Production "conceived and supervised" by Alfred Lunt and Lynn Fontanne. Scenery by Lee Simonson. Dances arranged by Morgan Lewis.

Original cast:

Dumpsty	George Meader
Signor Palota	Stephen Sandes
Donald Navadel	Barry Thomson
Pittaluga	S. Thomas Gomez
Auguste	Edgar Barrier
Captain Locicero	Edward Raquello
Dr. Waldersee	Sydney Greenstreet
Mr. Cherry	Bretaigne Windust
Mrs. Cherry	Jean Macintyre
Harry Van	Alfred Lunt
Shirley	Jacqueline Page
Beulah	Connie Crowell
Edna	Frances Foley
Francine	Etna Ross
Elaine	Marjorie Baglin
Bebe	Ruth Timmons
1st Officer	Alan Hewitt
2nd Officer	Winston Ross
3rd Officer	Gilmore Bush
4th Officer	Tomasso Tittoni
Quillery	Richard Whorf
Signor Rossi	Le Roi Operti
Signora Rossi	Ernestine De Becker
Major	Georgio Monteverde
Anna	Una Val
Irene	Lynn Fontanne

Achille Weber . . . . Francis Compton
Musicians . . . . . . Gerald Kunz, Max Rich, Joseph Knopf

The production ran for a total of 299 performances and won the Pulitzer Prize. A London production opened on 22 March 1938, starring Raymond Massey. That production ran for twenty-nine weeks.

A film version of the play was released by Metro–Goldwyn–Mayer in February 1939, using a screenplay by Sherwood. The film was produced by Hunt Stromberg and directed by Clarence Brown; it starred Clark Gable and Norma Shearer as Harry and Irene.

Kiss the Boys Good-bye

Opened 28 September 1939, at Henry Miller's Theatre, New York. A play in three acts by Clare Boothe [Luce]. Produced by Brock Pemberton. Directed by Antoinette Perry. Scenery by John Root.

Original cast:
Cindy Lou Bethany . . . . Helen Claire
Lloyd Lloyd . . . . Millard Mitchell
Madison Breed . . . . John Alexander
B. J. Wickfield . . . . Edwin Nicander
Leslie Rand . . . . Carmel White
Horace Rand . . . . Philip Ober
Herbert Z. Harner . . . . Sheldon Leonard
Top Rumson . . . . Hugh Marlowe
Myra Stanhope . . . . Benay Venuta
Maimie . . . . Ollie Burgoyne
George . . . . Frank Wilson

The production ran for 286 performances.

A musical film version of the play was released by Paramount in April 1941, using a screenplay by Harry Tugend and Dwight Taylor and directed by Victor Schertzinger. Music by Frank Loesser with lyrics by Victor Schertzinger and G. H. Clutson. The film starred Mary Martin, Don Ameche, and Oscar Levant.

Margin for Error

Opened 3 November 1939 at the Plymouth Theatre, New York. A satirical melodrama in two acts by Clare Boothe [Luce]. Produced by Richard Aldrich and Richard Myers. Directed by Otto Preminger. Scenery by Donald Oenslager.

Original cast:

Otto B. Horst	Philip Coolidge
Baron Max von Alvenstor	Bramwell Fletcher
Officer Moe Finklestein	Sam Levene
Frieda	Evelyn Wahle
Dr. Jennings	Bert Lytell
Sophie Baumer	Elspeth Eric
Karl Baumer	Otto Preminger
Thomas S. Denny	Leif Erickson
Captain Mulrooney	Edward McNamara

The production ran for 264 performances. A London production opened on 1 August 1940.

Twentieth Century–Fox bought the rights to the play in 1941 for a reported $25,000. The film was released in January 1943, using a screenplay by Lillie Hayward. The film was directed by Otto Preminger, who repeated his role as the Nazi consul. Joan Bennett was cast as Sophie Baumer and Milton Berle played Officer Finkelstein.

No Time for Comedy

Opened 17 April 1939 at the Ethel Barrymore Theatre, New York. A comedy in three acts by S. N. Behrman. Produced by the Playwrights' Company (S. N. Behrman, Elmer Rice, Maxwell Anderson, Sidney Howard, and Robert E. Sherwood) in association with Katharine Cornell. Directed by Guthrie McClintic. Settings by Jo Mielziner.

Original cast:

Linda Esterbrook	Katharine Cornell
Gaylord Esterbrook	Laurence Olivier
Amanda Smith	Margalo Gillmore
Philo Smith	John Williams
Robert	Peter Robinson
Makepeace Lovell	Robert Flemyng
Clementine	Gee Gee James

The production ran for 185 performances. A London production starring Rex Harrison and Lilli Palmer opened on 27 March 1941 and ran for eleven months.

A film version was released by Warner Brothers in 1940, produced by Jack Warner and Hal Wallis, directed by William Keighley. The screenplay was by Julius amd Philip Epstein. The film starred Rosalind Russell and Jimmy Stewart.

The Petrified Forest

Opened 7 January 1935 at the Broadhurst Theatre, New York. A play in two acts by Robert E. Sherwood. Produced by Gilbert Miller and Leslie Howard in association with Arthur Hopkins. Directed by Arthur Hopkins. Scenery by Raymond Sovey.

Original cast:

Gabby Maple . . . . Peggy Conklin
Gramp Maple . . . . Charles Dow Clark
Alan Squier . . . . Leslie Howard
Duke Mantee . . . . Humphrey Bogart
Boze Hertzlinger . . . . Frank Milan
Jason Maple . . . . Walter Vonnegut
Paula . . . . Esther Woodruff Leeming
Herb . . . . Robert Porterfield
Mrs. Chisholm . . . . Blanche Sweet
Mr. Chisholm . . . . Robert Hudson
Joseph . . . . John Alexander
Jackie . . . . Ross Hertz
Ruby . . . . Tom Fadden
Pyles . . . . Slim Thompson
Commander Klepp . . . . Aloysius Cunningham
Hendy . . . . Guy Conradi
Sheriff . . . . Frank Tweeddell
A Deputy . . . . Eugene Keith
Another Deputy . . . . Harry Sherwin
A Telegrapher . . . . Milo Boulton
Another Telegrapher . . . . James Doody

The play ran for 194 performances. A London production opened on 16 December 1942, at the Globe Theatre. That production starred Hartley Power as Duke Mantee and featured Constance Cummings, Owen Nares, Joyce Kennedy, and Douglas Jeffries.

A notable film version was released by Warner Brothers in February 1936, directed by Archie Mayo from a screenplay by Charles Kenyon and Delmar Daves. The film cast included Leslie Howard and Humphrey Bogart in their Broadway roles, but replaced Peggy Conklin with Bette Davis.

Rain from Heaven

Opened 24 December 1934, at the Golden Theatre, New York. "A comedy in three acts" by S. N. Behrman. Produced by the Theatre Guild, Inc. Directed by Philip Moeller. Scenery by Lee Simonson.

Original cast:

Joan Eldridge	Hancey Castle
Mrs. Dingle	Alice Belmore-Cliffe
Rand Eldridge	Ben Smith
Hobart Eldridge	Thurston Hall
Lady Violet Wyngate	Jane Cowl
Hugo Willens	John Halliday
Sascha Barashaev	Marshall Grant
Phoebe Eldridge	Lily Cahill
Clendon Wyatt	Statts Cottsworth
Nikolai Jurin	José Ruben

The play ran for 99 performances.

Reunion in Vienna

Opened 16 November 1931, at the Martin Beck Theatre, New York. A comedy in three acts by Robert E. Sherwood. Produced by the Theatre Guild, Inc. Directed by Worthington Miner. Scenery by Aline Bernstein.

Original cast:

Elena	Lynn Fontanne
Rudolf Maximilian Von Hapsburg	Alfred Lunt
Dr. Anton Krug	Minor Watson
Kathie	Mary Gildea
Ilse	Phyllis Connard
Emil	Lloyd Nolan

Herr Krug . . . . Henry Travers
Frau Lucher . . . . Helen Westley
Countess Von Stainz . . . . Virginia Chauvenet
Count Von Stainz . . . . Edward Fielding
Poffy . . . . Edouardo Ciannelli
Bedzi . . . . Bela Lublov
Strup . . . . Otis Sheridan
Torlini . . . . Bjon Koefoed
Police Inspector . . . . Murray Stevens
Chef . . . . Joseph Allen
Baroness Von Krett . . . . Cynthia Townsend
General Hoetzler . . . . Frank Kingdon
Talisz . . . . Owen Meech
Sophia . . . . Justina Wayne
Koeppke . . . . William R. Randall
Laundryman . . . . Stanley Wood
Valet . . . . Joseph Allenton
Bellboy . . . . Noel Taylor
Busboys . . . . Ben Kranz, Hendrik Booraem
Waiters . . . . Charles E. Douglas, George Lewis

The play ran for 280 performances. A London production opened at the Lyric on 3 January 1934. That production ran for six months.

A film version was released by Metro–Goldwyn–Mayer in 1933, with a screenplay by Ernest Vajda and Claudine West. It was directed by Sidney Franklin and starred John Barrymore and Diana Wynyard in the Lunt and Fontanne roles. Travers and Ciannelli were retained from the stage production.

The Time of Your Life

Opened 25 October 1939, at the Booth Theatre, New York. A comedy in three acts by William Saroyan. Produced by the

Theatre Guild, Inc., in association with Eddie Dowling. Directed by Eddie Dowling and William Saroyan. Scenery by Watson Barratt.

Original cast:

Joe	Eddie Dowling
Nick	Charles De Sheim
Tom	Edward Andrews
Kitty Duval	Julie Haydon
Newsboy	Ross Bagdasarian
Drunk	John Farrell
Willie	Will Lee
Tom	Edward Andrews
Dudley	Curt Conway
Harry	Gene Kelly
Wesley	Reginald Beane
Lorene	Nene Vibber
Blick	Grover Burgess
Arab	Houseley Stevens, Sr.
Mary L.	Celeste Holm
Krupp	William Bendix
McCarthy	Tom Tully
Kit Carson	Len Doyle
Nick's Ma	Michelette Burani
Sailor	Randolph Wade
Elsie	Cathie Bailey
A Killer	Evelyn Geller
Her Sidekick	Mary Cheffey
A Society Lady	Eva Leonard Boyne
A Society Gentleman	Ainsworth Arnold
First Cop	Randolph Wade
Second Cop	John Farrell

The production ran for 185 performances and the play was awarded the Pulitzer Prize and the New York Drama Critics' Circle Award. A London production opened at the Lyric,

Hammersmith, on 14 February 1946, with a cast featuring Margaret Johnston, Walter Crisham, and Irene Worth.

A film version was released by United Artists in 1948, produced by William and James Cagney, who had purchased the rights to the film from Saroyan for $150,000. The film starred James Cagney as Joe and featured William Bendix as Nick, Wayne Morris as Tom, Jeanne Cagney as Kitty Duval, and James Barton as Kit Carson.

Tobacco Road

Opened 4 December 1933 at the Masque Theatre, New York. A drama in three acts by Jack Kirkland, based on the novel by Erskine Caldwell. Directed and produced by Anthony Brown. Scenery by Robert Redington Sharpe.

Original cast:

Jeeter Lester	Henry Hull
Dude Lester	Sam Byrd
Ada Lester	Margaret Wycherly
Ellie Mae Lester	Ruth Hunter
Grandma Lester	Patricia Quinn
Lov Bensey	Dean Jagger
Henry Peabody	Ashley Cooper
Sister Bessie Rice	Maude Odell
Pearl Lester	Reneice Rehan
Captain Tim	Lamar King
George Payne	Edwin Walter

The production set a record for length of run, with a total of 3,182 performances. A less successful London production opened at the Gate Theatre on 19 May 1937.

Twentieth Century–Fox bought the rights to the play in 1940 for $150,000 and their film version was released in February 1941. The film was produced by Darryl F. Zanuck and directed by John Ford. The screenplay by Nunnally Johnson was adapted from Kirkland's play and based upon the Caldwell novel. Its cast included:

Jeeter Lester . . . . Charlie Grapewin
Sister Bessie . . . . Marjorie Rambeau
Elie Mae . . . . Gene Tierney
Dude Lester . . . . William Tracy
Ada Lester . . . . Elizabeth Patterson
Dr. Tim . . . . Dana Andrews
Peabody . . . . Slim Summerville
Lov . . . . Ward Bond
George Payne . . . . Grant Mitchell
Grandma . . . . Zeffie Tilbury
Chief of Police . . . . Russell Simpson

The Women

Opened 26 December 1936, at the Ethel Barrymore Theatre in New York. A comedy in three acts by Clare Boothe [Luce]. Produced by Max Gordon. Directed by Robert B. Sinclair. Scenery by Jo Mielziner.

Original cast:
Sylvia (Mrs. Howard Fowler) . . . . Ilka Chase
Nancy Blake . . . . Jane Seymour
Peggy (Mrs. John Day) . . . . Adrienne Marden
Edith (Mrs. Phelps Potter) . . . . Phyllis Povah
Mary (Mrs. Stephen Haines) . . . . Margalo Gillmore
Mrs. Morehead . . . . Jessie Busley

Crystal Allen . . . . Betty Lawford
Miriam Aarons . . . . Audrey Christie
Little Mary . . . . Charita Bauer
Jane . . . . Anne Teeman
Mrs. Wagstaff . . . . Ethel Jackson
Olga . . . . Ruth Hammond
First Hairdresser . . . . Mary Stuart
Second Hairdresser . . . . Jane Moore
Pedicurist . . . . Ann Watson
Euphie . . . . Eloise Bennett
Miss Fordyce . . . . Eileen Burns
First Saleswoman . . . . Doris Day
Second Saleswoman . . . . Jean Rodney
Head Saleswoman . . . . Lucille Fenton
First Model . . . . Beryl Wallace
Third Saleswoman . . . . Martina Thomas
A Fitter . . . . Joy Hathaway
Second Model . . . . Beatrice Cole
Princess Tamara . . . . Arlene Francis
Exercise Instructress . . . . Anne Hunter
Maggie . . . . Mary Cecil
Miss Watts . . . . Virgilia Chew
Miss Trimmerback . . . . Mary Murray
A Nurse . . . . Lucille Fenton
Lucy . . . . Marjorie Main
Countess de Lage . . . . Margaret Douglass
Helene . . . . Arlene Francis
Sadie . . . . Marjorie Wood
Cigarette Girl . . . . Lillian Norton

The production ran for 657 performances. A London production opened at the Lyric Theatre on 20 April and ran for 155 performances.

Clare Boothe Luce sold the film rights for the play in 1937 to Max Gordon's fledgling film production company for a hundred and twenty-five thousand dollars. Gordon consequently sold the rights to Metro–Goldwyn–Mayer, the company that ultimately produced the film and released it in September 1939. The screenplay by Anita Loos and Jane Murfin was adapted from the stage play. The film was directed by George Cukor and starred Norma Shearer as Mary Haines, Rosalind Russell as Sylvia Fowler, Paulette Goddard as Miriam Aarons, Joan Fontaine as Peggy Day, and Joan Crawford as Crystal Allen.

Notes

Introduction: Loving the Grotesque

1. "Long-Sought Gunman Slain by Police in Country Club," *New York Times*, 17 June 1935, p. 1.

2. "Fokine Home on Riverside Drive Ransacked; $25,000 in Loot Taken in Absence of Dancer"; "Two Die, Five Escape as Boat Capsizes"; "Boys Steal Pistol in Police Station, Rob and Kill Man," *New York Times*, 17 June 1935, p. 1.

3. The description of the archeological find is from Geoffrey Harpham, *On the Grotesque: Strategies of Contradiction in Literature* (Princeton: Princeton University Press, 1982), pp. 23–4. Reproductions of small segments of these frescoes appear in Harpham, p. 25; extensive verbal descriptions by the Renaissance critics can be found in Frances K. Barasch, *The Grotesque: A Study in Meanings* (The Hague: Mouton, 1971), pp. 19–20.

4. John Ruskin, *The Stones of Venice*, vol. III: *The Fall* (London: James Clark, 1851; reprint, New York: Merrill & Baker, 1895). Ruskin's was the first systematic analysis of the grotesque in this impressionistic "reading" of the design and architecture of past eras. In this third volume, Ruskin compares the grotesque designs of Venetian gargoyles in the "fallen" period of the late

Renaissance with earlier eras that in his view were marked by a higher spiritual, moral, and thus artistic cultural mood. His major distinction is between two types of grotesque: the "base" and the "noble." (In other references, he calls these types the "sportive" and the "terrible.") With a Victorian distaste for cynicism, Ruskin disparages the "idiotic mockery" of the "base" carvings with the confrontation with the awesomeness of eternity in the "terrible" or "noble" faces. The "noble" carvings are thus the reflection of a serious and profound civilization, whereas the "base" gargoyles display "an expression of low sarcasm which is . . . the most hopeless state into which the human mind can fall" (p. 122).

Wolfgang Kayser, *The Grotesque in Art and Literature,* translated by Ulrich Weisstein (Bloomington: Indiana University Press, 1963); first published in Germany as *Das Groteske: seine Gestaltung in Malerei und Dichtung* (Hamburg: Gerhard Stalling Verlag, 1957). Kayser sees the grotesque performing what amounts to a mystical task: performing a sort of exorcism of a culture's despair by first naming a horror and then deflating it with the comic. He also posits a "failed grotesque" that performs a malignant action by invoking a horror from out of commonplace experience and then leaving it undefeated, a type of "play with the absurd" that only makes us afraid of the "ghosts" it has "invoked" (p. 187).

Mikhail Bakhtin, *Rabelais and His World,* translated by Helene Iswolsky (Cambridge, Mass.: MIT Press, 1968); this book, although written in 1940, was not published until 1968 because it did not conform with approved methods of Soviet criticism. Bakhtin revised it to include a consideration of Kayser and others who had published in the intervening decades. In Bakhtin's view, the grotesque operates as an essential tool of folk culture, a weapon that uses the power of "carnival laughter" to deflate the dogmas and symbols of "official culture" (p. 12). The juxtaposition of these "serious" elements of the official culture within a context of folk humor creates the sensation of "a world inside out" in which the assumed power of the elite is mocked and derided by the folk (p. 11). Thus, for Bakhtin, the grotesque is a vehicle of transformation by which a world that has been frozen, reified by offical culture, can be thawed out and revived. The grotesque emerges in Bakhtin as a "liberating force" that "takes away all fears" through the "people's triumphant laughter" (pp. 24, 47).

Sigmund Freud, "The Uncanny" (1919), reprinted in *On Creativity and the Unconscious,* edited by Benjamin Nelson (New York: Harper & Row, 1958), pp. 123–61; and *Wit and Its Relation to the Unconscious,* translated by A. A. Brill, reprinted in *The Basic Writings of Sigmund Freud* (New York: Random House, 1938). Freud's classic essay on the "uncanny" and his chapter on the comic in his study of wit provide the starting point for several recent theorists of the grotesque. The most impressive of these is Michael Steig, "Defining the Grotesque: An Attempt at Synthesis," *Journal of Aesthetics and Art Criticism,* 29 (1970), pp. 253–60. Steig combines Freud's notion of a subconscious identification between *heimlich* and *unheimlich* with the psychologist's theory of the comic as a release of repressed "energy." He manages a unity between the apparently opposite psychological actions of these two phenomena – one that raises anxiety and one that releases it – in the notion of the grotesque. Steig argues that the defense work of the comic half of the grotesque object is only partially successful; its conflation with the uncanny at the same time spoils the therapeutic effect: "This is the basic paradox of the grotesque: it is double-edged; it at once allays and intensifies the effect of the uncanny; in pure comedy . . . the defense is complete and detachment is achieved" (p. 258). Anxieties, then, are not "defeated," but are constantly renewed as a natural part of human experience.

5. Flannery O'Connor, "Some Aspects of the Grotesque in Southern Fiction," in *Mystery and Manners: Occasional Prose,* edited by Sally and Robert Fitzgerald (New York: Farrar, Straus & Giroux, 1961), p. 40.
6. Tania Modleski, "The Terror of Pleasure: The Contemporary Horror Film and Postmodern Theory," in *Studies in Entertainment: Critical Approaches to Mass Culture,* Kathleen Woodward, general editor (Bloomington: Indiana University Press, 1986), pp. 155–66.

1. The Grotesque and the Great Depression

1. "New Deal Permanent, President Says; Asks Higher Pay, Shorter Hours, Now; Supreme Court Upholds Price Fixing," *New York Times,* 6 March 1934, p. 1.

2. Robert S. Lynd and Helen Merrell Lynd, *Middletown in Transition: A Study in Cultural Conflicts* (New York: Harcourt, Brace & World, 1937).

3. Though the identity of "Middletown" was revealed by the press in 1925, and even trumpeted by the town itself in billboards proclaiming it "The Ideal American City," the Lynds maintain a scientific distance from the place in the second study by referring to it consistently by its code name, Middletown, and its leading family (the Balls) as "the X family." See pp. 3–6 for the Lynds' description of the town's response to the first study.

4. It should not be overlooked, however, that grotesque art and artifacts were not the dominant work of the period. Far more attractive, and often of greater popularity, were objects of mass culture that ignored the tension and existed entirely within one "sphere" or the other – either in a world of the futurist or in a world of nostalgia. The thirties are, of course, famous in dramatic literature classes for the labor plays that were part of the decade's temporary animation of the American Left. Plays like *Waiting for Lefty* (Clifford Odets, 1935) or *Days to Come* (Lillian Hellman, 1936) presented no "civil war" between their own parts. For all their denunciation of the miseries of the present, the left-wing dramas of the thirties tended to be resolute in their convictions (capitalists are evil, workers are good) and supremely optimistic in their proffered solution: "Strike!" "The future, the future" the Marxist hero intones, no less frequently than did Buckminster Fuller. "Maybe we'll fix it," says Ralph in Odets's *Awake and Sing!* (1935), "so life won't be printed on dollar bills."

   On the unconflicted and conservative side were unrelievedly nostalgic texts, a few of which enjoyed long Broadway runs in the thirties. Plays such as *Life with Father* (Lindsay and Crouse, 1939), *Our Town* (Thornton Wilder, 1935), and the only play by Eugene O'Neill that could ever be called "beloved," *Ah, Wilder-*

ness! (1933), were essentially nostalgic resuscitations of a recently eclipsed historical moment when people rode in horsecars,
standards of moral decency were maintained, and, in brief,
everything was better.

   Both of these "seamless" types were shielded by a coating
of sentimentality. Future-looking pieces like William Cameron
Menzies's film of Wells's *Things to Come* (1936) or the essays of
Buckminster Fuller are as uncritical of scientific progress as *Life
with Father* is of the "good old days" with mom and dad, and
their ideological position is no less conservative. Both types
tended to assume traditional forms as well and so, by holding
up one piece of the cultural puzzle and declaring it to be the
whole thing, they fit easily into established and untroubling patterns of discourse. For an assessment of the cultural relations
among art, entertainment, and politics in the period, see Warren
Susman, *Culture and Commitment, 1929–1945* (New York: George
Braziller, 1973).

5. Margaret Mitchell, *Gone with the Wind* (New York: Macmillan,
   1936), pp. 1023–4.

6. Mystification is an essential part of the success of Mitchell's
   strategy. The "old days" that Tara and Mammy symbolize were,
   of course, brutal and oppressive times in which a few Scarlett
   O'Haras enjoyed a materially easy life at the expense of millions
   of impoverished whites and enslaved blacks. The very apotheosis of patriarchal capitalism, built upon an artifice of "chivalry"
   that kept women out of power and provided the social excuses
   for the ownership of human beings, the "old days" of Scarlett's
   youth are presented by Mitchell in a haze of country twilights
   and magnolia blossoms, an orderly and idyllic time of "good"
   slaveholders (like the O'Haras) and "bad" ones (those who beat
   their slaves). The oppression of women and the institution of
   slavery are made acceptable in the thought of the narrative by
   Mitchell's insistence on special "codes" that gave these people
   far more power than logic would have led one to assume. The
   oppression of women is obfuscated by the persistent depiction of
   the "wily wife" (like Mrs. O'Hara or Melanie Wilkes) who really rules the household by manipulating her husband. Similarly,

in the world of *Gone with the Wind*, slavery is encased in Mitchell's belief that most slaves preferred slavery over freedom and that they – like the wily wives – lived within a secret "pact" with their owners that allowed them to exercise authority and to express their views within the "codes" of mumbling and the pretence of ignorance.

7. *New York Times*, 1 July 1934, p. 1.
8. *New York Times*, 10 August 1934, p. 1.
9. This and the following quotations are from "Hitler Forecasts No Reich Overturn in Next 1,000 Years," *New York Times*, 6 September 1934, p. 1.
10. From the text of Roosevelt's first inaugural address as printed in the *New York Times*, 5 March 1933, p. 1.
11. This and the following quotation from Roosevelt's second inaugural address as printed in the *New York Times*, 21 January 1937, p. 1.
12. "Primo's Son Fights Sword Duel with Captain; Both Slightly Wounded in Second Encounter," *New York Times*, 4 March 1930, p. 1.
13. "Fire Damages Sagamore Hill, Roosevelt Home; President's Widow Gives Alarm as Roof Burns," *New York Times*, 23 January 1931.
14. "'American Buddha' Died Heartbroken in India; Feared Healing Power Lost with Spectacles," *New York Times*, 21 December 1930, p. 1.
15. "Walker Back Today but Wants No 'Fuss'," *New York Times*, 21 September 1931, p. 1.
16. "Moses Bids Casino Quit Central Park," *New York Times*, 24 May 1934, p. 1.
17. Robert E. Sherwood, Preface to *Reunion in Vienna* (New York: Scribner's, 1931), pp. vii–ix.
18. By the end of the decade, when Sherwood had entered the Roosevelt administration, his plays had taken on a far more positive and activist turn. A more detailed discussion of the plays and Sherwood's evolving spirit is found in Chapter 2.
19. The most literal playing out of this theme was in the 1937 Leo McCarey film *Make Way for Tomorrow*, the story of an old cou-

ple who find themselves penniless and obsolete in modern America. The social systems that had supported their parents in their old age have crumbled, and their children have scattered geographically. The couple finds that they must split up to survive, and they move in with separate children, superficial and hustling "modern" people from whom they feel strangely alienated.

20. Arthur Schlesinger, Jr., "When the Movies Really Counted," *Show*, 3 (April 1963), p. 77.

21. Stephen B. Oates, *William Faulkner: The Man and the Artist* (New York: Harper & Row, 1987), p. 109.

22. Apparently, the screenplay was also based on an adaptation by journalist-playwright John L. Balderston of a stage play by Peggy Webling. *The International Dictionary of Films and Filmmakers*, vol. 1, *Films*, edited by Christopher Lyon (New York: Perigee, 1985), p. 160. Balderston had earlier collaborated with Hamilton Deane on the Broadway production of *Dracula*.

23. Earlier film versions of Robert Louis Stevenson's *Dr. Jekyll and Mr. Hyde* include one directed by F. W. Murnau (1920) and another starring John Barrymore (1921). *Haliwell's Filmgoer's and Video Viewer's Companion*, ninth edition (New York: Perennial, 1990), p. 350. American stage adaptations had included that by Thomas Russell Sullivan for Richard Mansfield (1887). Arthur Hobson Quinn, *A History of the American Drama: From the Civil War to the Present Day*, second edition (New York: Appleton–Century–Crofts), 1936, vol. 1, p. 294.

24. So impressed was Irving Thalberg with the financial success of Tod Browning's *Dracula* in 1931 that he allowed the director a free hand in production of his next film. In 1932, the worst year of the depression, Browning assembled a cast recruited largely from sideshow attractions and made a film that, in its outline, is a simple melodrama of a "normal" woman who marries a midget for his money and then flaunts her affair with the circus strongman. The "freaks" eventually become so fed up with the cruelty and pretensions of the "normal" people that they pursue them and exact a severe punishment.

The disruptive effect of Browning's film lies not in its narrative but in its images. The "freaks" possess astonishing qualities that are displayed in a matter-of-fact attitude by the camera and performers. Some of the actors have misshapen heads; others have prehensile feet or no limbs at all; still others are midgets or Siamese twins. The "freaks" are shown as dignified and sensitive people who come together in a crisis, a clear contrast to the vanity and stupid preening of Cleopatra and Hercules, the "normal" performers in the circus. The film thus overturns the usual voyeuristic pleasure of looking at beautiful bodies and instead challenges the viewer to go beyond the titillation of peeping at people with abnormalities, admit one's fascination, and take a long look. The camera lingers patiently, cutting only from a medium shot to a close-up and back to a medium shot, as Rodian (the Living Torso) lights a cigarette using only his mouth. The Armless Woman fills most of the frame in a protracted shot of her in conversation, but the focus of the shot is not her face but her eating and drinking by use of her feet.

25. Joanna E. Rapf, "What Do They Know in Pittsburgh?: American Comic Film in the Great Depression." *American Humor*, 3 (Summer–Fall 1984), pp. 187–99.

26. Antonin Artaud, *The Theatre and Its Double*, in *Antonin Artaud: Selected Writings,* translated by Helen Weaver, edited by Susan Sontag (New York: Farrar, Straus & Giroux, 1976), p. 241.

27. Susan Stewart, *Nonsense: Aspects of Intertextuality in Folklore and Literature* (Johns Hopkins University Press: Baltimore, 1979).

28. Quotes here and below are from Ephraim Katz, *The Film Encyclopedia* (New York: G. P. Putnam's Sons, 1979), p. 934.

29. The concepts of "resonance" and "cultural frame" are developed clearly and concisely in Michael Schudson, "How Culture Works: Perspectives from Media Studies on the Efficacy of Symbols," *Theory and Society* (March 1989), pp. 153–80.

2. The Political Analogy; or, "Tragicomedy" in an In-Between Age

1. Quoted in John Mason Brown, *The Worlds of Robert E. Sherwood, Mirror to His Times: 1896–1939* (New York: Harper & Row, 1962), p. 332.

2. Thomas Mann, "Conrad's *The Secret Agent,*" in *Past Masters and Other Papers,* translated by Helen T. Lowe-Porter (1933; reprint, Freeport, N.Y.: Books for Libraries Press, 1968), pp. 240–1; Mann's statement is the cornerstone for William Van O'Connor in his *The Grotesque: An American Genre, and Other Essays* (Carbondale: Southern Illinois University Press, 1962).

3. I see no point in distinguishing between "tragicomedy," which implies an alternation of discrete bits of comedy and tragedy in the work of art, and "black comedy" or "dark comedy," with their focus on the ambivalent response on the part of the audience. The terms seem to me to be different ways of describing what is essentially the same aesthetic phenomenon.

4. In choosing Muncie as an exemplar of middle-class taste, I follow the example of Robert S. Lynd and Helen Merrell Lynd, *Middletown in Transition: A Study in Cultural Conflicts* (New York: Harcourt, Brace & World, 1937), discussed in Chapter 1.

5. Friedrich Dürrenmatt's theatre essays of the 1950s laid out a systematic argument for the necessity of this kind of symbolic portrayal of chaos if theatre is to be relevant in this century: "We can achieve the tragic out of comedy. We can bring it forth as a frightening moment, as an abyss that opens suddenly. . . . The grotesque is only a way of expressing in a tangible manner, of making us perceive physically the paradoxical, the form of the unformed, the face of a world without a face." From his "Problems of the Theatre" (1955), translated by Gerhard Nellhaus in *European Theories of the Drama,* rev. ed., edited by Barrett H. Clark (New York: Crown, 1965), pp. 316–17.

6. These statistics reflect my own evaluation of the plays that appear in the "Calendar of Productions" in Samuel L. Leiter, *The Encyclopedia of the New York Stage, 1930–1940* (New York: Greenwood Press, 1989), pp. 943–78.

7. Quoted here and below from Friedrich Dürrenmatt, "Note on Comedy" (1952), translated by H. M. Waidson, in *Writings on Theatre* (London: Jonathan Cape, 1976), pp. 57–8.

8. Brooks Atkinson, "Idiot's Delight," *New York Times,* 25 March 1936.

9. Brooks Atkinson, "R. E. Sherwood's *Idiot's Delight* Receives Annual Award," *New York Times,* 10 May 1936, section 10, p. 1.

10. Malcolm Goldstein, *The Political Stage: American Drama and Theater of the Great Depression* (New York: Oxford University Press, 1974), p. 351.

11. C. W. E. Bigsby, *A Critical Introduction to Twentieth-Century American Drama*, vol. 1: *1900–1940* (Cambridge: Cambridge University Press, 1982), p. 145.

12. Brenda Murphy, *American Realism and American Drama, 1880–1940* (Cambridge: Cambridge University Press, 1987), p. 173.

13. Brown, *Worlds of Robert E. Sherwood*, p. 319.

14. Robert E. Sherwood, Preface to *There Shall Be No Night* (New York: Scribner's, 1940), pp. xviii–xix.

15. Robert E. Sherwood, Preface to *Reunion in Vienna* (New York: Scribner's, 1931), pp. vii–xvi.

16. Robert E. Sherwood, *The Petrified Forest* (New York: Scribner's, 1935), p. 62.

17. Arthur Hobson Quinn (1875–1960), the aging representative of a previous generation, was puzzled and appalled by the incongruous qualities of *The Petrified Forest*. He found that the play violated tenets of probability in realism. His remarks are reminiscent of classical arguments about "decorum" in drama (meaning that characters should exhibit only those qualities that are deemed appropriate to their "station" in life): "The climax of absurdity is reached by the advent of a gang headed by a cold blooded person who alone is able to appreciate the noble action of the poet in begging to shoot him in order that his life insurance may be paid to the young woman! The confused critical standards of today need no better example than the praise accorded to this play. If it had frankly been a burlesque, it would have at least been amusing. But in the endowing of a murderer, who does not even care about the lives of his own men, with an imaginative reach to which he would of course be a stranger, there was a deliberate falsity of tone which is hard to forgive." Arthur Hobson Quinn, *A History of the American Drama: From the Civil War to the Present Day*, second edition (New York: Appleton–Century–Crofts), 1936, p. 296.

18. A remark to Lucius Beebe of the *Herald Tribune*, quoted in Brown, *Worlds of Robert E. Sherwood*, p. 319.

19. Quoted in ibid., p. 330.
20. Robert E. Sherwood, typescript and notes for *Idiot's Delight,* Lilly Library, Indiana University (Bloomington).
21. Quoted in Brown, *Worlds of Robert E. Sherwood,* p. 338.
22. The designer Walter Dorwin Teague wrote in 1939: "We have reverted again to a primitive state of human development. We are primitives in this new machine age. We have no developed history behind us to use in our artistic creations." Quoted in Martin Greif, *Depression Modern: The Thirties Style in America* (New York: Universe Books, 1975), p. 34.
23. This description of the Guild's "culinary theatre" comes from Goldstein, *The Political Stage,* p. 340. Complete listings of the Guild's productions in the thirties and detailed information about the board's activities can be found in Roy S. Waldau, *Vintage Years of the Theatre Guild, 1928–1939* (Cleveland: Case Western Reserve University Press, 1972). More exact figures on expenditures and income of Guild productions is available in Thomas Gale Moore, *The Economics of the American Theater* (Durham, N.C.: Duke University Press, 1968) and, for the first two years of the decade, in Alfred L. Bernheim, *The Business of the Theatre: An Economic History of the American Theatre, 1750–1932* (New York: Benjamin Blom, 1932). The Guild's papers are collected in the Beinecke Library, Yale University.
24. Theatre Guild founding motto quoted in Walter Prichard Eaton, *The Theatre Guild: The First Ten Years* (New York: Brentano's, 1929), p. 5.
25. Harold Clurman, *The Fervent Years: The Group Theatre and the Thirties* (New York: Da Capo Press, 1983), p. 26; Clurman is, of course, far from being an objective commentator on the Guild, since his assessment comes as part of his justification for starting the Group Theatre. I find his arguments generally convincing if for no other reason than that so many intelligent theatre people of the period were persuaded by him at the time. Actors such as Franchot Tone and Morris Carnovsky, playwrights such as John Howard Lawson and Maxwell Anderson, all of whom had been Guild talent, were moved enough to offer their future services to the Group. Moreover, a reading of Theresa Helburn's

autobiography *(A Wayward Quest,* Boston: Little, Brown, 1960) and the correspondence and board minutes reproduced by Waldau in *Vintage Years,* confirms the well-meaning but "dilettantish" attitudes described by Clurman.

26. Theatre Guild program for *Idiot's Delight,* 1936, Billy Rose Collection, New York Public Library at Lincoln Center.

27. The average run figure is rounded up from the exact one of 70.8; the source is Moore, *Economics of the American Theater,* p. 152.

28. Waldau, *Vintage Years,* pp. 232, 249.

29. Regarding Ruskin's "noble grotesque," see Introduction, n. 4. For Bosanquet, see Dale Jacquette, "Bosanquet's Concept of Difficult Beauty," *Journal of Aesthetics and Art Criticism* (Fall 1984): 79–87.

30. "Introduction," in Clare Boothe [Luce], *Kiss the Boys Good-bye* (New York: Random House, 1939), pp. vii–xx.

31. Heywood Broun, "Kiss the Bourgeoisie Good-Bye," *New Republic,* 26 October 1938, p. 331.

32. Harry Hansen, "The First Reader," *New York World-Telegram,* 27 January 1939.

33. Heywood Broun, "It Seems to Me," *New York World-Telegram,* 3 February 1939.

34. Richard Lockridge, *"Margin for Error," New York Sun,* 4 November 1939. Other reviewers of interest are Kelcey Allen, *"Margin for Error," Women's Wear Daily,* 4 November 1939; John Mason Brown, *"Margin for Error* by Clare Boothe," *New York Evening Post,* 4 November 1939; Burns Mantle, *"Margin for Error," New York Daily News,* 4 November 1939; Arthur Pollock, *"Margin for Error* Makes Melodrama Out of German Doings Here," *Brooklyn Eagle,* 4 November 1939; Richard Watts, Jr., *"Margin for Error," New York Herald Tribune,* 4 November 1939.

35. Sidney B. Whipple, *"Margin for Error* Opens at Plymouth," *New York World-Telegram,* 4 November 1939.

36. Walter Winchell, "Another Boothe Play Scores Hit with Audience," *New York Daily Mirror,* 4 November 1939.

37. Henry R. Luce, Introduction to *Margin for Error* (New York: Random House, 1940), p. x.

38. The obituary that William F. Buckley wrote for Clare Boothe Luce is a fine example of sentimental hagiography. See "Clare Boothe Luce, RIP," *National Review*, 6 November 1987, pp. 20–2.

39. Clare Boothe [Luce], Foreword to *The Women* (New York: Random House, 1937), pp. ix, xii.

40. Wilfrid Sheed published a lively précis of his biography of Boothe in *Harper's*, February 1982. Diverse perspectives on the political meaning of her work are found in Buckley, "Clare Boothe Luce, RIP," and John Kenneth Galbraith, "An Affectionate Portrait of Clare Luce," review of *Clare Boothe Luce*, by Wilfrid Sheed (1982), *Saturday Review* (February 1982), pp. 56–8.

41. John Mason Brown, "*Kiss the Boys Good-bye* at the Henry Miller's," *New York Post*, 29 September 1938.

42. Boothe [Luce], Foreword to *The Women*, p. xii.

43. Quoted by Stephen Shadegg, *Clare Boothe Luce: A Biography* (New York: Simon & Schuster, 1970), p. 193.

44. This and the following quotation from the *Congressional Record*, 9 February 1943, vol. 89, pt. 1, pp. 761, 763, respectively.

45. Hepburn was asked to comment on Luce's speech in the course of an interview with Theodore Strauss of the *New York Times* (21 February 1943, section B). She called Luce's newly coined word "downright cheap claptrap," an example of "the kind of cleverness that goes with fancy shoes and chic." Hepburn dismissed Luce's remark as a "silly, meaningless wisecrack" intended to bring down someone who was sincere in trying to bring about a better world.

46. Shadegg, *Clare Boothe Luce*, p. 195.

47. Clare Boothe Luce, "The High Human Price of Detente," *National Review*, 11 November 1977, p. 1291.

48. For a summary of Luce's career, plays, and the connections between her political activities and literary work, see Mark Fearnow, *Clare Boothe Luce: A Research and Production Sourcebook* (Westport: Greenwood Press, 1995).

49. Clare Boothe Luce, *The Women* ("Newly Revised by the Author") (New York: Dramatists Play Service, 1966).

50. Joseph Wood Krutch, *The American Drama since 1918: An In-formal History* (New York: Random House, 1939), p. 198.

51. Among Behrman's plays of the 1930s: *Brief Moment* (1931), *Biography* (1932), *Rain from Heaven* (1934), *End of Summer* (1936), *Wine of Choice* (1938), and *No Time for Comedy* (1939); the last mentioned is the notable exception to this formula. *No Time for Comedy* does include a "fascinating" woman, but the problem of the woman is superseded by the issue of the artist (her husband) and his struggle to write comedy in a world in turmoil and despair. This problem, a side issue in the other plays, takes the place of the usual wooing pattern: Now the artist is wooed, on the one hand by the mistress who hopes to make him be what he is not (a "profound" writer), and on the other hand by his wife, who wants him to rely on his "natural" characteristics – skeptical intelligence and good humor – and keep on writing comedies in the face of the gloom. The analogy for America still holds.

52. S. N. Behrman, *End of Summer* (New York: Random House, 1936), p. 241.

53. S. N. Behrman, *The Burning Glass* (New York: Little, Brown, 1968), pp. 38–44.

54. Kenneth T. Reed, *S. N. Behrman* (Boston: Twayne Publishers, 1975), p. 17.

55. Krutch, *American Drama since 1918*, p. 181.

56. This kind of displacement of a playwright by history is a bit different from the more obvious case of "topical" plays whose usefulness passes as culture moves on to other issues. Rachel Crothers is a prime example of this dynamic on the American scene; her issue-oriented plays made her one of the leading figures of the commercial stage in the 1920s, but as women's rights progressed and the desperate causes of the 1930s took over the national mentality, her work gradually faded from view. Behrman's plays do not elucidate specific issues but embody an entire cultural situation. He has more in common with Racine than with Galsworthy or even Ibsen.

57. William Saroyan, "Memories of the Uppression," *Literary Review* (Fall 1983), pp. 9–11.

58. Lahr calls *Blithe Spirit* "a paradigm of survivor guilt. . . . In the end, Condomine engineers a victory over the ghosts, and puts fear, guilt, and mourning behind him." John Lahr, *Coward the Playwright* (London: Methuen, 1982), pp. 116–17.
59. *"Arsenic and Old Lace," PM,* 11 January 1941.
60. Quoted in Burns Mantle, *The Best Plays of 1940–41* (New York: Dodd, Mead & Company, 1941), p. 165.
61. This and the following quoted in William Manchester, *The Glory and the Dream: A Narrative History of America, 1932–1972* (Boston: Little, Brown & Company, 1973), pp. 225–6.
62. Results of a Gallup poll, given in Manchester, *Glory and the Dream,* p. 228.
63. Joseph Kesselring, *Arsenic and Old Lace* (New York: Dramatists Play Service, 1941), p. 91.
64. Garry Wills, "Total War," introduction to *Scoundrel Time* by Lillian Hellman (Boston: Little, Brown & Company, 1976), pp. 3–34.

3. Misery Burlesqued: The Peculiar Case of Tobacco Road

1. See "Revolutionary Realism," in Ira A. Levine, *Left-wing Dramatic Theory in the American Theatre* (Ann Arbor: UMI Research Press, 1985), pp. 113–28.
2. A substantial number of publicity photographs are on file as part of the Billy Rose Collection of the New York Public Library at Lincoln Center. Many of the same photographs appear in the Collection's set of souvenir programs and publicity flyers for the play. Among the captioned photos from a souvenir program is one showing Jeeter and Lov standing by a fence. Ellie Mae is leaning over the fence and leering at Lov. Jeeter (Henry Hull) is scratching his head in a stereotypically comic gesture, indicating stupidity. The caption reads: "Why don't you take her?" / "No, I want Pearl!" Another photo shows Jeeter in his underwear above a caption reading, "Where ya going with my

pants?" This incident is not part of the script as published in 1934 nor does it appear in later revisions.

3. Factual information, such as dates of run and number of performances, is taken from Samuel L. Leiter, *The Encyclopedia of the New York Stage, 1930–1940* (New York: Greenwood Press, 1989).

4. The production benefited from the publicity generated by the many attempts by mayors and judges to ban *Tobacco Road* from being performed in their cities. Kirkland claimed that he retained a lawyer whose sole occupation was seeking injunctions to prevent the closing of the production in various cities on the road. The most famous of the banning incidents, persistently reported by the New York press, was in Chicago, where – after a run of some seven weeks in 1935 – Mayor Frank Kelly came to see the production. Kelly walked out, declaring the play obscene, and ordered it closed. When the order was overturned by the courts, Kelly kept the play out of the city by threatening to revoke the license of any theatre that housed it. In an attempt to get past Kelly's restrictions, Kirkland opened a production on the showboat *Dixieana*, moored in Lake Michigan at Michigan City, Indiana. This production closed when, in 1938, the boat was rammed by a Coast Guard cutter and sank. The ramming was apparently accidental. Other notable banning fights took place in Detroit, Omaha, New Orleans, Albuquerque, Oklahoma City, Albany, and Newark. See Sidney Shallett, "Infinity via *Tobacco Road*," *New York Times*, 10 March 1940.

5. "*Road* Closing August 17 after Record Run," *Variety*, 24 July 1940. The article points out that while *Tobacco Road* held the record for the longest run, *Abie's Irish Rose* (1922) held the record for profitability, with a net income of $5 million.

6. Danton Walker, "Prodigal's Return," an article that appeared in the souvenir program of the play as revived in 1942. Leiter, *Encyclopedia of the New York Stage*, mentions a start-up cost of $3,500 (p. xxx) but does not list a source for the figure. It seems unlikely that Kirkland and Goldreyer would have inflated the figure upward as this would have made the profitability of the play slightly less impressive.

7. These prices appear in numerous advertisements in the New York newspapers and in flyers for the touring companies that are available in the clipping files of the Billy Rose Collection, New York Public Library at Lincoln Center. The New York prices were below those of most Broadway shows (which averaged between $3 and $5, according to Leiter, *Encyclopedia of the New York Stage*, p. xxvii) and were the reason for *Tobacco Road*'s lagging behind *Abie's Irish Rose* in profitability. The earlier play had run for 2,327 performances, compared with 3,182 for *Road*, but the former had commanded substantially higher prices throughout its run in the prosperous twenties.

8. Leiter, *Encyclopedia of the New York Stage*, p. 438.

9. Goldreyer released numerous photographs of the several actresses who played Ellie Mae, showing the "real" appearance of each next to her appearance as Ellie Mae. Several of the photographs suggest that the actress is nude except for a sheet draped over the shoulder. These photographs are available in the Billy Rose Collection, New York Public Library at Lincoln Center, as are the clippings and program notes cited here as publicity myths.

10. Quoted from a flyer advertising the tour of the company featuring John Barton to Indianapolis, undated, Billy Rose Collection, New York Public Library at Lincoln Center.

11. "He Must Have Liked It," *New York Times*, 8 June 1941.

12. Lloyd Lewis, "Whither *Tobacco Road?*" *New York Times*, 30 November 1941.

13. Jack Kirkland, "How Long *Tobacco Road?*" *New York Times*, Drama Section, 12 January 1939.

14. The play did receive essentially negative reviews from Robert Garland (*New York World-Telegram*), Gilbert Gabriel (*New York American*), and John Mason Brown (*New York Post*). However, it was reviewed rather favorably by three of the most respected critics of the day: Brooks Atkinson of the *New York Times*, George Jean Nathan (*Vanity Fair*, 2 February 1934), and Joseph Wood Krutch (*Nation*, 137, p. 718). Krutch's review, later incorporated into his *The American Drama since 1918* (Random House, 1939), is an impressive consideration of the grotesque in the the-

atre as a contrast to traditional forms and their aesthetic contracts.

15. Erskine Caldwell, "A Note about *Tobacco Road*," as Preface to
    Tobacco Road, adapted for the stage by Jack Kirkland (New
    York: Viking, 1934), n.p.

16. Kenneth Burke, "Caldwell: Maker of Grotesques," in *The Phi-
    losophy of Literary Form: Studies in Symbolic Action* (Baton
    Rouge: Louisiana State University Press, 1967), pp. 350–60;
    a recent article by another critic makes an artful case for Cald-
    well's skillfulness in using humor in the novel *Tobacco Road* as
    a form of rebuke to callous readers: See Robert H. Brinkmeyer,
    Jr., "Is That You in the Mirror, Jeeter?: The Reader and *To-
    bacco Road*," *Pembroke Magazine*, 11 (1979), pp. 47–50.

17. Caldwell seems to have been a writer whose work consistently
    "turned out" (in terms of the public's response) to be rather
    different from his intentions for it. Throughout the long run of
    Tobacco Road, just as in his remarks about *God's Little Acre* and
    the *Tobacco Road* novel, Caldwell insisted that the work present-
    ed a documentary picture of life. On several occasions, when
    acquaintances scoffed at the "reality" of the play, he offered to
    drive them to Georgia immediately so that he could show them
    real-life Lesters. No one is recorded as having accepted.

    Caldwell engaged in a public debate (through newspaper col-
    umns) about the accuracy of the "conditions" in the play with
    Representative Brasswell Deen of Georgia. Caldwell accused
    Deen and other Southern politicians of maintaining a "coolie
    serfdom" across the region. See "Of *Tobacco Road*: Mr. Cald-
    well Defends the Character of Jeeter Lester and His Family,"
    New York Times, Drama Section, 10 May 1936.

18. Kenneth Burke, *Permanence and Change: An Anatomy of Purpose*
    (New York: New Republic, 1935), p. 69.

19. William Manchester, *The Glory and the Dream: A Narrative
    History of America, 1932–1972* (Boston: Little, Brown & Compa-
    ny, 1973), p. 248.

20. All three incidents from Manchester, *Glory and the Dream*, pp.
    248–9.

21. Kirkland revived the play in 1942, 1947, and in 1950 (with an African–American cast), but none of these revivals achieved notable runs.

22. The surprising, unframed cartooning that animated *Tobacco Road* did appear in flashes in other successful productions of the period. Sidney Kingsley's *Dead End* (1935), for example, worked a kind of therapy on culture's fear of gangsters and urban crime, as *Tobacco Road* did for the fear of impoverishment. The burlesque potential of the piece found a kind of playing out in the "big picture" of the entertainment industry as the desperate boys of *Dead End* went on to become the comic buffoons known as the Dead End Kids and, later, the Bowery Boys.

    Clifford Odets stumbled into some unintentional grotesqueries in his rapid composition of *Till the Day I Die* (1935). The play is so extreme and repetitious in its moments of violence that it threatens to become a black comedy. Its brief action (about thirty minutes) contains some dozen beatings of innocent and heroic persons; a scene of homosexual seduction by a sadistic Nazi; and the suicides of two of the few admirable characters. With some minor alterations and skillful acting, the play might have offered the anxiety-reducing cultural therapy for the fear of rising dictatorships that *Tobacco Road* offered for the fear of poverty. As a serious drama, it found no resonance. Instead, the play has often been criticized for being forced and artificial.

    Among other flashes of unintentional burlesque in the period were the catalog of abuses in Elmer Rice's *We, the People* (1933); the travesty of treacheries and suicides that makes up his *Judgment Day* (1934); and the sadistic doctor in John Howard Lawson's *Marching Song* (1937), slavering over the torture of the hero by use of a hot poker and screaming out, "Kill him! Kill him!"

23. *New York Times*, News Section, 23 November 1938.

24. Bosley Crowther, "*Tobacco Road*," *New York Times* film review of 21 February 1941, reprinted in *New York Times Film Reviews*, vol. 3, pp. 1771–2.

25. Nunnally Johnson, "Temporary Script" for *Tobacco Road*, dated 6 November 1940; memorandum titled, "Conference with Mr.

Zanuck on Temporary Script," dated 23 November 1940; these items are part of the John Ford Collection at the Lilly Library of Indiana University, Bloomington, Indiana, Box 4, Folder 18.

26. In an interview with Dan Ford (John Ford's grandson) during the 1970s, Nunnally Johnson claims to have gone onto the set of *Tobacco Road* to challenge Ford on his casting of "a bunch of wild Irishmen" in the roles of "hookworm Southerners"; Johnson saw this casting as part of a generally mistaken, "unrealistic" direction in which Ford was taking the film. According to Johnson, Ford was unmoved. He concludes the story by saying that the film was both a critical and financial failure and that this lack of authenticity may have been a reason. At any rate, Ford's casting was "a complete mistake." Nunnally Johnson, transcript of an interview with Dan Ford, John Ford Collection of the Lilly Library, Box 12, Folder 8, p. 5.

27. Mulvey's essay, built around her idea of woman as image and man as bearer of the look, illustrates vividly the tendency of the director to shoot the woman full-front, as an object of beauty, whereas the man is typically shot at oblique angles and in shadow. See Laura Mulvey, "Visual Pleasure in Narrative Cinema," in *Women and the Cinema*, edited by Karyn Kay and Gerald Peary (New York: Dutton, 1977).

4. Chaos and Cruelty in the Theatrical Space: Horse Eats Hat, Hellzapoppin, and the Pleasure of Farce

1. Psychologist quote: 5 July 1936; songs listed in William Manchester, *The Glory and the Dream: A Narrative History of America, 1932–1972* (Boston: Little, Brown & Company, 1973), p. 150; Fibber McGee and Molly quote from montage in ibid., p. 123; "Hurry please," quoted in ibid., p. 194.

2. Robert Sherwood, Preface to *Reunion in Vienna* (New York: Scribner's, 1931), pp. xiv–xv.

3. Letter to Robert Haas, in *Selected Letters of William Faulkner*, edited by Joseph Blotner (New York: Random House, 1977), p. 125.

4. Eric Bentley, *The Life of the Drama* (New York: Atheneum, 1964), p. 244.

5. Albert Bermel, *Farce* (New York: Simon & Schuster, 1982), p. 21.

6. See Richard France, *The Theatre of Orson Welles* (Lewisburg, Pa.: Bucknell University Press, 1977), p. 88; and John Houseman, *Run-through* (New York: Simon & Schuster, 1972), p. 223.

7. Connelly quoted in John O'Connor and Lorraine Brown, *Free, Adult, Uncensored: The Living History of the Federal Theatre Project* (London: Methuen, 1980), p. 43.

8. Watts quoted in Samuel L. Leiter, *The Encyclopedia of the New York Stage, 1930–1940* (New York: Greenwood Press, 1989), p. 340.

9. Orson Welles and Edwin Denby, *Horse Eats Hat*, playscript collection of the Federal Theatre Project Archives, Music Division of the Library of Congress, p. II-8.

10. Leiter, *Encyclopedia of the New York Stage*, p. 339.

11. Houseman, *Run-through*, p. 221.

12. This and the preceding quotations are from ibid., p. 222.

13. Bentley, *Life of the Drama*, p. 226.

14. France, *Theatre of Orson Welles*, p. 83.

15. This and the following Gabel quote from ibid., p. 88.

16. Interestingly, Edward Albee, with his well-known admiration for the European "Absurdists," has said that *Hellzapoppin* was his "favorite play" as a boy and that he went to see it "several times." From an informal conversation with Mr. Albee, 8 February 1990.

17. Factual information about the production is available in Leiter, *Encyclopedia of the New York Stage*, pp. 321–2, and in the files of clippings and programs in the Billy Rose Collection, New York Public Library at Lincoln Center. Unfortunately, the vast majority of the clippings from this era were not identified by date or even by newspaper.

18. The film was directed by H. C. Potter. See *Hellzapoppin* in *New York Times Film Reviews* for 26 December 1941.

19. This "aqua" production had Olsen and Johnson sharing the bill with various divers, swimmers, and nightclub entertainers. See

program file in the Billy Rose Collection, New York Public Library at Lincoln Center.

20. Brooks Atkinson, Review of *Hellzapoppin*, *New York Times*, 23 September 1938.

21. This summary of disruptions was gleaned from reviews and, especially, from a graphic illustration of the events of the evening and their locations that appeared in the *New York Herald Tribune*, 26 March 1939.

22. Photographs of these Barto and Mann routines are available in the *Hellzapoppin* files in the Billy Rose Collection, New York Public Library at Lincoln Center.

23. The source of this photo spread is not identified in the clipping file of the Billy Rose Collection, New York Public Library at Lincoln Center.

24. Bentley, *Life of the Drama*, p. 255.

25. From a clipping entitled "Murder in 46th Street," source unidentified, Billy Rose Collection, New York Public Library at Lincoln Center.

26. Ole Olsen, interview with Jack Gould, "Two Swedes Explode on Broadway," newspaper and date unidentified, Billy Rose Collection, New York Public Library at Lincoln Center.

27. Bentley, *Life of the Drama*, p. 245.

28. John Anderson, "*Hellzapoppin*'s Stars (S)chatter a Column: Or Critic Prints a Bang-Up Letter," *New York Journal*, undated clipping in Billy Rose Collection, New York Public Library at Lincoln Center.

29. Robert S. McElvaine offers a convincing story of the thirties as a time of personal and social redemption in *The Great Depression: America, 1929–1941* (New York: Times Books, 1984).

30. Antonin Artaud, *The Theatre and Its Double*, in *Antonin Artaud: Selected Writings*, translated by Helen Weaver, edited by Susan Sontag (New York: Farrar, Straus & Giroux, 1976), p. 241. See also the section "Film Farce" in Chapter 1 of the present volume.

31. Joseph Wood Krutch, *The American Drama since 1918: An Informal History* (New York: Random House, 1939), p. 254. The exception to this "containment effect" in farce is the lingering disruptive effect of politically focused farces, such as those of

Joe Orton or Dario Fo. These playwrights present very specific social targets for attack. Both Orton and Fo frequently focus on the police, who are stripped down – sometimes quite literally – and suffer a consequent diminution in the audience's eyes. The effect may be a lessening of the power their real-life counterparts wield in the minds of those who have seen the play. Still, the effect is one of private liberation rather than mass synthesis.

32. Warren Susman, *Culture and Commitment, 1929–1945* (New York: George Braziller, 1973), pp. 15–16.

Bibliography

Albee, Edward. Interview by author. Hanover, Indiana, 8 February 1990.

Allen, Kelcey. "*Margin for Error.*" *Women's Wear Daily*, 4 November 1939.

"'American Buddha' Died Heartbroken in India; Feared Healing Power Lost with Spectacles." *New York Times*, 21 December 1930, p. 1.

Artaud, Antonin. "The Theatre and Its Double." In *Antonin Artaud: Selected Writings*, translated by Helen Weaver, edited by Susan Sontag. New York: Farrar, Straus & Giroux, 1976, pp. 215–76.

Atkinson, Brooks. Review of *Arsenic and Old Lace. New York Times*, 11 January 1941.

Review of *Hellzapoppin. New York Times*, 23 September 1938.

Review of *Idiot's Delight. New York Times*, 25 March 1936.

"R. E. Sherwood's *Idiot's Delight* Receives Annual Award." *New York Times*, 10 May 1936, section 10, 1.

Bakhtin, Mikhail. *Rabelais and His World*, translated by Helene Iswolsky. Cambridge: MIT Press, 1968.

Barasch, Frances K. *The Grotesque: A Study in Meanings*. The Hague: Mouton, 1971.

Behrman, S. N. *The Burning Glass*. Boston: Little, Brown, 1968.

End of Summer. New York: Random House, 1936.

Bentley, Eric. *The Life of the Drama.* New York: Atheneum, 1964.

Bermel, Albert. *Farce.* New York: Simon & Schuster, 1982.

Bernheim, Alfred L. *The Business of the Theatre: An Economic History of the American Theatre, 1750–1932.* New York: Benjamin Blom, 1932.

Bigsby, C. W. E. *Twentieth-Century American Drama,* vol. 1: *1900–1940.* Cambridge: Cambridge University Press, 1982.

"Boys Steal Pistol in Police Station, Rob and Kill Man." *New York Times,* 17 June 1935, p. 1.

Brinkmeyer, Robert H., Jr. "Is That You in the Mirror, Jeeter?: The Reader and *Tobacco Road.*" *Pembroke Magazine,* 11 (1979), pp. 47–50.

Bronner, Edwin J. *The Encyclopedia of the American Theatre: 1900–1975.* New York: A. S. Barnes, 1980.

Broun, Heywood. "It Seems to Me." *New York World-Telegram,* 3 February 1939.

   "Kiss the Bourgeoisie Good-Bye." *New Republic,* 26 October 1938, p. 331.

Brown, John Mason. "*Kiss the Boys Good-bye* at the Henry Miller's." *New York Post,* 29 September 1938.

   "*Margin for Error* by Clare Boothe." *New York Evening Post,* 4 November 1939.

   The Worlds of Robert E. Sherwood, Mirror to His Times: 1896–1939. New York: Harper & Row, 1962.

Buckley, William F. "Clare Boothe Luce, RIP." *National Review,* 6 November 1987, pp. 20–2.

Burke, Kenneth. *Permanence and Change: An Anatomy of Purpose.* New York: New Republic, 1935.

   The Philosophy of Literary Form: Studies in Symbolic Action. Baton Rouge: Louisiana State University Press, 1967.

Caldwell, Erskine. "A Note about *Tobacco Road.*" Preface to play version adapted by Jack Kirkland. New York: Viking, 1934.

   "Of *Tobacco Road:* Mr. Caldwell Defends the Character of Jeeter Lester and His Family." *New York Times,* Drama Section, 10 May 1936.

Clurman, Harold. *The Fervent Years: The Group Theatre and the Thirties.* 1945. Reprint, New York: Da Capo Press, 1983.

Conkle, E. P. *Prologue to Glory.* In *Federal Theatre Plays,* edited by Pierre de Rohan. New York: Random House, 1938, pp. 1–81.

Crowther, Bosley. Review of *Tobacco Road. New York Times* film review of 21 February 1941. Reprinted in *New York Times Film Reviews*, vol. 3, pp. 1771–2.

Dürrenmatt, Friedrich. "Problems of the Theatre," translated by Gerhard Nellhaus. In *European Theories of the Drama*, rev. ed., edited by Barrett H. Clark. New York: Crown, 1965, pp. 313–18.

Writings on Theatre and Drama, translated by H. M. Waidson. London: Jonathan Cape, 1976.

Eaton, Walter Prichard. *The Theatre Guild: The First Ten Years.* New York: Brentano's, 1929.

Faulkner, William. *Selected Letters of William Faulkner*, edited by Joseph Blotner. New York: Random House, 1977.

Fearnow, Mark. *Clare Boothe Luce: A Research and Production Sourcebook*. Westport, Conn.: Greenwood Press, 1995.

Fergusson, Francis. *The Idea of a Theater*. Princeton: Princeton University Press, 1949.

"Fire Damages Sagamore Hill, Roosevelt Home; President's Widow Gives Alarm as Roof Burns." *New York Times*, 23 January 1931.

"Fokine Home on Riverside Drive Ransacked; $25,000 in Loot Taken in Absence of Dancer." *New York Times*, 17 June 1935, p. 1.

France, Richard. *The Theatre of Orson Welles*. Lewisburg, Pa.: Bucknell University Press, 1977.

Freud, Sigmund. "The Uncanny." 1919. Reprinted in *On Creativity and the Unconscious*, edited by Benjamin Nelson. New York: Harper & Row, 1958, pp. 253–60.

Wit and Its Relation to the Unconscious, translated by A. A. Brill. Reprinted in *The Basic Writings of Sigmund Freud*. New York: Random House, 1938, pp. 633–803.

Galbraith, John Kenneth. "An Affectionate Portrait of Clare Luce." Review of *Clare Boothe Luce*, by Wilfrid Sheed (1982). *Saturday Review* (February 1982), pp. 56–8.

Gianetti, Louis, and Scott Eyman. *Flashback: A Brief History of Film*. Englewood Cliffs: Prentice–Hall, 1986.

Goldstein, Malcolm. *The Political Stage: American Drama and Theater of the Great Depression*. New York: Oxford University Press, 1974.

Goodman, Arthur. *If Booth Had Missed*. New York: Samuel French, 1932.

Greif, Martin. *Depression Modern: The Thirties Style in America*. New York: Universe Books, 1975.

Hansen, Harry. "The First Reader." *New York World-Telegram*, 27 January 1939.

Harpham, Geoffrey. *On the Grotesque: Studies of Contradiction in Literature*. Princeton: Princeton University Press, 1982.

Heidegger, Martin. *Poetry, Language, Thought*, translated by Albert Hofstadter. New York: Harper & Row, 1971.

"He Must Have Liked It." Article about return visits to *Tobacco Road* performances. *New York Times*, Drama Section, 8 June 1941.

Hellzapoppin. *New York Times Film Reviews*, 26 December 1941.

"Hitler Forecasts No Reich Overturn in Next 1,000 Years." *New York Times*, 6 September 1934, p. 1.

Horace. "The Art of Poetry," translated by C. Smart. Reprinted in *European Theories of the Drama*, edited by Barrett Clark, revised edition New York: Crown, 1965, pp. 24–32.

Houseman, John. *Run-through*. New York: Simon & Schuster, 1972.

Hugo, Victor. Preface to *Cromwell*. 1827. Reprinted in *European Theories of the Drama*, edited by Barrett Clark, revised edition New York: Crown, 1965, pp. 357–8.

Jacquette, Dale. "Bosanquet's Concept of Difficult Beauty." *Journal of Aesthetics and Art Criticism* (Fall 1984), pp. 79–87.

Johnson, Nunnally. "Conference with Mr. Zanuck." Memorandum dated November 23, 1940. John Ford Collection, Lilly Library of Indiana University, Bloomington, Ind., Box 4, Folder 18.

Interview with Dan Ford. Transcript from taped conversation. John Ford Collection, Lilly Library of Indiana University, Bloomington, Ind., Box 12, Folder 8.

Tobacco Road, "Temporary Script" for film. Dated 6 November 1940. John Ford Collection, Lilly Library of Indiana University, Bloomington, Ind., Box 4, Folder 18.

Katz, Ephraim. *The Film Encyclopedia*. New York: G. P. Putnam's Sons, 1979.

Kayser, Wolfgang. *The Grotesque in Art and Literature*, translated by Ulrich Weisstein. Bloomington: Indiana University Press, 1963.

Kesselring, Joseph. *Arsenic and Old Lace*. New York: Dramatists Play Service, 1941.

Khouri, Nadia. "The Grotesque: Archeology of an Anti-Code." *Zadadnienia Radzajow Literackich*, 23 (1980), pp. 3–24.

Kirkland, Jack. "How Long *Tobacco Road*?" *New York Times*, 12 January 1939.

Krutch, Joseph Wood. *The American Drama since 1918*. New York: Random House, 1939.

Lahr, John. *Coward the Playwright*. London: Methuen, 1982.

Leiter, Samuel L. *The Encyclopedia of the New York Stage, 1930–1940*. New York: Greenwood Press, 1989.

Levine, Ira A. *Left-wing Dramatic Theory in the American Theatre*. Ann Arbor: UMI Research Press, 1985.

Lewis, Lloyd. "Whither *Tobacco Road?*" *New York Times*, 30 November 1941.

Lockridge, Richard. "*Margin for Error*." *New York Sun*, 4 November 1939.

"Long-Sought Gunman Slain by Police in Country Club." *New York Times*, 17 June 1935, p. 1.

Luce, Clare Boothe. Foreword to *The Women*. New York: Random House, 1937, pp. ix–xxi.

    "The High Human Price of Detente." *National Review*, 11 November 1977, 1291.

    Introduction to *Kiss the Boys Good-bye*. New York: Random House, 1937, pp. vii–xx.

    Speech to Congress. *Congressional Record*, 9 February 1943, vol. 89, pt. 1, pp. 759–64.

    The Women ("Newly Revised by the Author"). New York: Dramatists Play Service, 1966.

Luce, Henry R. Introduction to *Margin for Error*. New York: Random House, 1940, pp. vi–xx.

Lynd, Helen Merrell, and Robert S. Lynd. *Middletown in Transition: A Study in Cultural Conflicts*. 1937. Reprint, San Diego: Harcourt, Brace, Jovanovich, 1982.

McElvaine, Robert S. *The Great Depression: America, 1929–1941*. New York: Times Books, 1984.

Manchester, William. *The Glory and the Dream: A Narrative History of America, 1932–1972*. Boston: Little, Brown & Company, 1973.

Mann, Thomas. "Conrad's *The Secret Agent*." In *Past Masters and Other Papers*, translated by Helen T. Lowe-Porter. 1933. Reprint, Freeport, N.Y.: Books for Libraries Press, 1968.

Mantle, Burns. "*Margin for Error*." *New York Daily News*, 4 November 1939.

Meyerhold, Vsevolod. "Balagan." Reprinted in Edward Braun, *Meyerhold on Theatre*. New York: Hill & Wang, 1969, pp. 119–43.

Mitchell, Margaret. *Gone with the Wind*. New York: Macmillan, 1936.

Modleski, Tania. "The Terror of Pleasure: The Contemporary Horror Film and Postmodern Theory." In *Studies in Entertainment: Critical Approaches to Mass Culture,* edited by Tania Modleski, pp. 155–66. *Theories of Contemporary Culture 7,* Kathleen Woodward, general editor. Bloomington: Indiana University Press, 1986.

Moore, Thomas Gale. *The Economics of the American Theater.* Durham, N.C.: Duke University Press, 1968.

Mulvey, Laura. "Visual Pleasure in Narrative Cinema." In *Women in the Cinema,* edited by Karyn Kay and Gerald Peary. New York: Dutton, 1977, pp. 412–28.

"Murder in 46th Street." Unidentified clipping in the alphabetical clipping file on *Hellzapoppin,* Billy Rose Theatre Collection, New York Public Library at Lincoln Center.

Murphy, Brenda. *American Realism and American Drama, 1880–1940.* Cambridge: Cambridge Unversity Press, 1987.

"New Deal Permanent, President Says; Asks Higher Pay, Shorter Hours, Now; Supreme Court Upholds Price Fixing." *New York Times,* 6 March 1934, p. 1.

Oates, Stephen B. *William Faulkner: The Man and the Artist.* New York: Harper & Row, 1987.

O'Connor, Flannery. "Some Aspects of the Grotesque in Southern Fiction." In *Mystery and Manners: Occasional Prose,* edited by Sally and Robert Fitzgerald. New York: Farrar, Straus & Giroux, 1961, pp. 36–50.

O'Connor, John, and Lorraine Brown. *Free, Adult, Uncensored: The Living History of the Federal Theatre Project.* London: Methuen, 1980.

O'Connor, William Van. *The Grotesque: An American Genre, and Other Essays.* Carbondale: Southern Illinois University Press, 1962.

Olsen, Ole. "Two Swedes Explode on Broadway." Interview with Jack Gould. Newspaper and date unidentified. Clipping file, Billy Rose Theatre Collection, New York Public Library at Lincoln Center.

Pollock, Arthur. "*Margin for Error* Makes Melodrama Out of German Doings Here," *Brooklyn Eagle,* 4 November 1939. Clipping file, Billy Rose Theatre Collection, New York Public Library at Lincoln Center.

"Primo's Son Fights Sword Duel with Captain; Both Slightly

Wounded in Second Encounter." *New York Times*, 4 March 1930, p. 1.

Quinn, Arthur Hobson. *A History of the American Drama: From the Civil War to the Present Day*, second edition. New York: Appleton–Century–Crofts, 1936.

Rabkin, Gerald. *Drama and Commitment: Politics in the American Theatre of the Thirties*. Bloomington: Indiana University Press, 1964.

Rapf, Joanna. "What Do They Know in Pittsburgh?: American Comic Film in the Great Depression." *American Humor* (Summer–Fall 1984), pp. 187–99.

Reed, Kenneth T. *S. N. Behrman*. Boston: Twayne Publishers, 1975.

"*Road* Closing August 17 after Record Run." *Variety*, 24 July 1940.

Roosevelt, Franklin Delano. First Inaugural Address. Reprinted in *New York Times*, 5 March 1933, p. 1.

Second Inaugural Address. Reprinted in *New York Times*, 21 January 1937, p. 1.

Ruskin, John. *The Stones of Venice*, vol. III: *The Fall*. 1851. Reprint, New York: Merrill & Baker, 1895.

Saroyan, William. "Memories of the Uppression." *Literary Review* (Fall 1983), pp. 9–11.

Schlesinger, Arthur, Jr. "When the Movies Really Counted." *Show* (April 1963), pp. 75–9.

Schudson, Michael. "How Culture Works: Perspectives from Media Studies on the Efficacy of Symbols." *Theory and Society*. (March 1989), pp. 153–80.

Shadegg, Stephen. *Clare Boothe Luce: A Biography*. New York: Simon & Schuster, 1970.

Shallett, Sidney. "Infinity via *Tobacco Road*." *New York Times*, 10 March 1940.

Sheed, Wilfrid. "Clare Boothe Luce: What a Woman Had to Do to Make It in the American Century." *Harper's* (February 1982), pp. 22–38.

Sherwood, Robert E. *Abe Lincoln in Illinois*. New York: Scribner's, 1937.

The Petrified Forest. New York: Scribner's, 1935.

Preface to *Reunion in Vienna*. New York: Scribner's, 1931, pp. vii–xvi.

Preface to *There Shall Be No Night*. New York: Scribner's, 1940, pp. ix–xxx.

Smith, Wendy. *Real Life: The Group Theatre and America, 1931–1940.* New York: Knopf, 1990.

Steig, Michael. "Defining the Grotesque: An Attempt at Synthesis." *Journal of Aesthetics and Art Criticism,* 29 (1970), pp. 253–60.

Stewart, Susan. *Nonsense: Aspects of Intertextuality in Folklore and Literature.* Baltimore: Johns Hopkins University Press, 1979.

Strauss, Theodore. "Sweetness and Light: Katharine Hepburn Proves That One May Be Not Only Forthright but Charming." *New York Times,* 21 February 1943, section B.

Susman, Warren. *Culture and Commitment, 1929–1945.* New York: George Braziller, 1973.

Thompson, John O. *Monty Python: Complete and Utter Theory of the Grotesque.* London: British Film Institute Press, 1982.

Thompson, Philip. *The Grotesque.* London: Methuen, 1972.

"Two Die, Five Escape as Boat Capsizes." *New York Times,* 17 June 1935, p. 1.

Uruburu, Paula M. *The Gruesome Doorway: An Analysis of the American Grotesque.* New York: Peter Lang, 1987.

Waldau, Roy S. *Vintage Years of the Theatre Guild, 1928–1939.* Cleveland: Case Western Reserve University Press, 1972.

Walker, Danton. "Prodigal's Return." Article in a souvenir program from *Tobacco Road.* 1942. Program file, Billy Rose Theatre Collection, New York Public Library at Lincoln Center.

Watts, Richard, Jr., *"Margin for Error," New York Herald Tribune,* 4 November 1939. Clipping file, Billy Rose Theatre Collection, New York Public Library at Lincoln Center.

Welles, Orson, and Edwin Denby. *Horse Eats Hat.* 1936. Playscript collection of the Federal Theatre Project Archives, Music Division of the Library of Congress, 113 Madison Building, Washington, D.C.

West, Nathanael. *A Cool Million.* In *The Complete Works of Nathanael West.* New York: Farrar, Straus & Giroux, 1971.

"What Happens and Where at the Madhouse, '*Hellzapoppin*'." Illustration in the *New York Herald Tribune,* 26 March 1939.

Whipple, Sidney. "*Margin for Error* Opens at Plymouth." *New York World-Telegram,* 4 November 1939.

Wills, Garry. "Total War." Introduction to *Scoundrel Time,* by Lillian Hellman. Boston: Little, Brown & Company, 1976, pp. 3–34.

Winchell, Walter. "Another Boothe Play Scores Hit with Audience." *New York Daily Mirror,* 4 November 1939.

Index

DATE DUE